Single-Session Therapy and Getting Unstuck

Single-Session Therapy and Getting Unstuck

Focused Help with Emotional Blocks

Windy Dryden, PhD

Onlinevents Publications

First edition published by Onlinevents Publications

Copyright (c) 2025 Windy Dryden and Onlinevents Publications

Windy Dryden
136 Montagu Mansions, London W1U 6LQ

Onlinevents Publications
38 Bates Street, Sheffield, S10 1NQ
www.onlinevents.co.uk
help@onlinevents.co.uk

A catalogue record of this book is
available from the British Library.

First edition 2025

ISBN: 978-1-914938-51-1

Contents

1

Introduction

This Book

This book focuses on my single-session therapy work with people who have sought help for issues with which they feel stuck.

The people whose sessions appear in this book were recruited through Onlinevents, an organisation that offers online training and CPD events for counsellors and therapists. They responded to a posting that explained that I would be offering a complimentary single session to those struggling with an issue with which they were stuck, hence the book's title.

Single-Session Therapy

Therapy is not a one-size-fits-all activity. It can be practised in different arenas – with individuals, couples, families and groups and the amount of time people spend 'in therapy' varies tremendously – from one session to many years. This is a challenge for the training of therapists, as we will see. While single-session therapy (SST) can be practised with individuals, couples, and families, this book will focus on single-session work with individual adults. In ordinary clinical practice, single-session therapy is a contractual method of working with the client, aimed at helping the individual achieve the outcome they seek from the session. It is understood that after the session, the individual engages in a reflective process, considering what they have learned, digesting this learning, implementing it, and allowing time to pass. At this stage, they are best placed to determine if they require further assistance. Therefore, unless the client is suicidal, at risk, or in crisis at the end of the session, they are not offered another appointment at that time.

Therefore, in general, single-session therapy is a misnomer as the client is not confined to a single session. However, in this book, the clients whose therapy sessions are presented and discussed understood that they were volunteering for a single session to address a particular adversity or issues with which they felt stuck. Thus, I was only offering them one session with no expectation of further assistance from me.

I have been offering single therapy sessions to a diverse array of individuals for over a decade and have come to recognise that much can be accomplished from a single therapeutic conversation when several important factors are present:

- The therapist must be convinced of the therapeutic potential of single-session therapy and demonstrate enthusiasm for this mode of therapy delivery to the client.
- The client needs to comprehend the nature of single-session therapy and recognise what they can realistically achieve from the session, as well as what they cannot.

- Both the client and therapist are focused on helping the client achieve the outcome of the session specified and wanted by the client.
- The therapist helps the client to articulate what help they are looking for and provides this help for the client with the client's hoped-for outcome clearly in mind. This is shown in Figure 1.1.

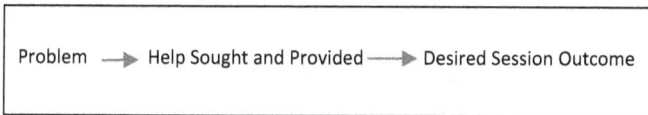

Problem ➝ Help Sought and Provided ➝ Desired Session Outcome

Figure 1.1 Problem, help and session outcome

Whenever possible, the client is encouraged to prepare for the session to help them get the most from it.

In general, during their initial education, therapists are trained to provide ongoing therapy to clients. If they are trained to offer brief therapy, it typically follows a six-session model. Currently, therapists are not educated to provide single-session therapy, despite data from therapy agencies indicating that the most common number of visits clients made to these agencies is 'one' (the mode) – see Brown and Jones (2005) and Young (2018).

The Single-Session Mindset with Implications for Practice

In the work presented in this book, my practice is guided by elements of what has been termed the single-session therapy mindset or single-session thinking (Hoyt, Young and Rycroft, 2021). These elements are particularly relevant to the work presented here – single-session therapy where the client is not offered further sessions, at least from me.

It Is Possible for Me to Conduct a Session Without Prior Knowledge of the Person

I know nothing about the volunteer other than that they have volunteered for a session and what they have written on their pre-session questionnaire (see below). I am happy to proceed with a single session once I am clear that the person wants one, has given informed consent to proceed, and has realistic expectations about what they can achieve from the session. These two conditions are met in each of the eight single sessions discussed in this book

Potentially, Anyone Can Be Helped in a Single Session

As, potentially anyone can be helped in a single session, there is no need to conduct an assessment of the client's suitability for SST. In my work for this book, my approach could be described as open access. No barriers to having the session were in place. However, just because anyone can be helped in SST, does not mean that everyone will be helped in this mode of therapy

I Focus on the Person, Not on the Disorder

If someone who come for a single session of therapy mentions that they are suffering from a psychological disorder, I ask them how they think this might impact on the help that I provide them in the session. From my perspective, I am focused on what the person wants from the session rather than on what they have been diagnosed with. Indeed, if ten people diagnosed with an emotionally unstable personality disorder come to SST for help they are all likely to want to take away different things, some of which I may be able to help them with and some not.

I Establish with the Person that We Share a Common Understanding of the Session's Purpose

If the person has a different understanding of the session's purpose, one that does not focus on a personal issue they want help with, then we don't proceed. Thus, one volunteer mistakenly thought I was offering a single session of supervision rather than a single session of therapy. When I explained what the purpose of the session was from my perspective, they decided not to proceed.

I Provide Therapy from Moment One

The person and I get down to the business of helping the client achieve their desired outcome from the session straightaway. I do not undertake a case history, an assessment of the client or a case formulation. It is not that I do not value these activities, but they do not have a major role in the practice of SST.

I View the Session as a Whole, Complete in Itself

The session is not a prelude to further help. It has a beginning phase, a middle phase and an ending phase and is complete in itself.

The Person and I Agree to Focus on the Issue with which the Person Feels Stuck. Once Established, the Focus Needs to Be Maintained

As mentioned above, the people whose work I discuss in this book volunteered for help either with a specific issue with which they felt stuck. Generally, this issue became the focus of the ensuing conversation.

Once this focus had been established, it was my responsibility to ensure that it was maintained. However, sometimes, in SST it transpires that a new focus, which is more meaningful to the client, emerges, and I will shift to this focus if guided by the client. If the original focus remains relevant, I may need to interrupt the client to keep us both on track. In such cases, the best way to do so is to offer the client a rationale for interrupting them and to ask for permission to proceed. If this is granted, I seek to discover from the client how I may best do so.

I Clarify the Person's Goal for the Session, and the Therapeutic Work Is Devoted to its Achievement

Many, but not all, therapists in ongoing therapy ask their clients to identify their end-of-therapy goals. However, few ask them what their end-of-session goals are. Since I am only seeing the person once, it makes sense for me to ask the volunteer for the latter. Once the session goal has been agreed upon, the work is devoted to helping the person achieve this goal.

I Endeavour to Establish a Working Alliance with the Client Promptly

In my experience with SST, the working alliance can be established promptly and maintained throughout the session. First, I establish that the person and I are on the same page concerning the purpose of our conversation (shared 'views' of the working alliance, Dryden, 2011). I then strive to work collaboratively with them to help them achieve the outcome that they want from the session. This is known as the 'goals' domain of the working alliance (Bordin, 1979). Additionally, I strive to understand the person's nominated issue from their perspective (empathy), am transparent with them (also known as genuineness) – see below – and strive to help them feel understood (empathy). I also strive to help them see that there is hope that they can get unstuck from the issue with which they presently feel stuck. By showing them that I am taking their nominated issue seriously and am prepared to work with their goals, I believe that I am showing them respect. Finally, as the session proceeds, we will discover shared ways of working that we will help them person walk away feeling that they have something new to think about and/or implement. This represents the 'task domain' of the working alliance.

Finally, I think that my enthusiasm for SST and my keenness to help the person helps to form the working alliance in SST.

There is some research that shows that those clients who have formed a good working alliance with their therapists in SST have a better outcome from the session than those who have not formed a good working alliance with theirs (Simon, Imel, Ludman and Steinfeld, 2012).

I Endeavour to Be Transparent

There are several ways in which I demonstrate transparency in SST. First, I am clear about what SST is and what it isn't. Second, I am clear about what I can and cannot do in the session. Finally, I will answer any questions the person has as honestly as possible.

Single-Session Therapy is Client-Led

This is arguably one of the most important features of the SST mindset. When clients are assessed for the suitability of therapy, the assessor typically leads in determining which approach serves the client's best interest. In contrast, when someone volunteers for a single session as outlined in this book, they make their own decision that SST is appropriate for them, and I am pleased to support this. Additionally, the client takes the initiative by identifying an issue to discuss during the session, suggesting a focus for the session, and expressing what they would like to achieve by the end of it, all of which I am happy to accommodate unless doing so would be harmful to the person.

Some SST therapists employ a specific approach to single-session work, such as narrative therapy (Cooper, 2024) or chairwork (Pugh, 2024) and apply it to all clients. While clearly under the heading of 'single-session therapy', such approaches tend to be therapist-led in terms of the *tasks* domain of the working alliance, even though they are client-led in the *goals* domain of the alliance.

I Identify and Meet the Client's Preference for Being Helped

While most people seeking single-session help are looking for an effective way of addressing a specific issue, this is by no means the only help that they seek (Dryden, 2025a). Consequently, it is critical to establish at the outset what help a person is seeking from the session. Here are the major forms of help that people tend to seek from SST. I tend to ask a person to select the main oner form of help that they are seeking.

- Help me develop a greater understanding of the issue
- Help me by just listening while I talk about the issue
- Help me to feel heard and understood
- Help me express my feelings about the issue
- Help me solve an emotional or behavioural problem; help me get unstuck
- Help me make a decision
- Help me resolve a dilemma
- Help me by signposting me to the most appropriate service for my situation

Sometimes a person really wants to get unstuck from an issue, but states that they want a different form of help. Here is an example:

Counsellor: So, you want to discuss your feelings of guilt about your mother. Is that right?

Client: Yes, that's correct.

Counsellor: What help do you need from me regarding this issue?

Client: I want you to help me understand my feelings of guilt better.

Counsellor: And if you understand your feelings of guilt better, what do you hope that this understanding will lead to?

Client: I hope it will lead to me finding a way of addressing my guilt feelings more effectively.

In this vignette, the client initially declares that they want to understand an issue better, but it transpires that such understanding in the person's mind leads to a hoped-for resolution of the problem.

A Complex Problem Does Not Always Require a Complex Solution

It is often thought that a therapist in single-session therapy only has time to help the person deal with a fairly simple, clear-cut problem, and there is insufficient time to address a complex issue. However, it is possible to help a person take the first step to deal with a complex problem, and in doing so, the problem may become less complex and the person's efficacy in addressing it may increase setting in train a virtuous cycle of change.

I Focus on What the Client Has Done Before Concerning the Problem and Other Issues

One thing is clear. When someone seeks help for a problem with which they are stuck, then they will have made previous attempts to deal with the issue. While it is apparent that these attempts have not been wholly successful, since the person still has the issue, it may be that some of these attempts may have yielded some benefit for the person and if so, the client can use these helpful elements in creating a solution to the problem.

I also want to discover what successes the person has had in addressing other emotional problems, both similar and dissimilar to the problems with which they are stuck, since the person and I may be able to make use of some of these effective strategies in dealing with the stuck issue.

I Focus on the Client's Internal Strengths and External Resources

There are two phrases which I keep in mind when doing single-session work. These are: (i) 'There is nothing wrong with you that what's right with you can't cure' and

(ii) 'Only you can do it, but you don't have to do it alone.' The first phrase serves as a reminder for me to help the person identify the strengths they possess that can assist in overcoming their identified problem. The second phrase serves as a reminder for me to help the person identify resources in their environment that they can also use to get unstuck from the problem.

I Keep in Mind that I Need to Use Different Methods with Different Clients

Single-session therapy is not an approach to therapy in the way that CBT, person-centred therapy, or psychodynamic therapy is. Rather, it represents a method of therapy delivery. This indicates that therapists from diverse approaches can practise SST. Furthermore, it implies that a therapist may well need to utilise different methods with various clients, depending on their goals and the type of assistance they seek.

I Am Solution-Focused, if Relevant

As I said earlier, while most people who come to single-session therapy do so because they are looking for a solution to an emotional problem with which they are stuck (Dryden, 2025a), this is not universally the case. Thus, I do not assume that I will adopt a solution-focused approach in every session, but I am prepared to do so if that aligns with what the client seeks as an outcome to the session. When helping the client to construct a solution, I use the following sources:

- The opposite to the factors that have served to maintain the problem with which they are stuck
- Helpful features from the person's previous attempts to solve the nominated problem before
- What has helped when the person client has solved both related and unrelated problems before
- The person's strengths. I think of these as either tough-minded or tender-minded
- Helpful external resources
- Role models
- The person's views on what will help
- My views on what will help

When helping the client to select a solution then the main criterion is that the person can integrate it into their life.

Types of solution

When helping a client find a solution, I have in mind the following types of solution:

- *A frame change solution* (also known as reframing). Here I help someone by encouraging them to put an adversity into a different frame. For example, encouraging someone to look at these salient matters from a different time perspective.
- *An inference change solution.* Here, I help a person by helping them to re-intent an adversity so that it is no longer an adversity. For example, when I help a person to see what they thought was their mother's intrusiveness was just her usual way of starting a conversation.

- *An attitude change solution.* Here, I help a person develop, for example, a flexible attitude towards an adversity rather than a rigid attitude.
- *A behavioural change solution.* Here, I help a person change their behaviour towards a person with whom they are struggling to see if this makes that person's behaviour less of an adversity.
- *An environmental change solution.* Here, the person decides to change the environment in which the adversity is located. For example, leaving a job where the person is being bullied.
- *A combination of the above solutions.*

I Encourage the Person to Rehearse the Selected Solution, if Feasible

If the client is seeking a solution to their nominated problem, then if it is feasible to do so, I encourage them to rehearse the solution to see how it feels to implement it and to determine if they can imagine implementing it in their own life. In doing so, I will use role play, imagery and chairwork. However, if there is not enough time to do such rehearsal or if doing so might overwhelm the person, then I will skip this step.

I Help the Person Develop an Action Plan

An action plan clarifies several key parameters related to implementing their selected solution in their life. Ideally, it should spell out:

- *Why* the person is going to implement the solution
- *What* the person is going to do in implementing the solution

- *Where* the person is going to implement the solution
- *Which* adversities will the person face in implementing the solution
- *Who* will be present when the person implements the solution
- *How* often is the person going to implement the solution

However, in reality, I find that I only have time to discuss the most salient of these factors with the person.

I Help the Person Identify and Deal with Potential Obstacles to the Execution of the Action Plan

Before leaving the action plan, it is helpful to ask the person to consider potential obstacles to their execution of this plan. Once I have helped the person to identify these obstacles, we work together to problem-solve ways to overcome them using imagery to encourage the person to picture themself doing so.

Small May Be Beautiful

If people think that the goal of single-session therapy is to render the person's problem a non-problem by the end of the session, then they have misunderstood its purpose. I am not saying that a person will never leave a session with their problem completely solved but it is not common. When it does occur, the person is able to make a reframe in the session that does not need to be rehearsed outside the session and which does seem to have solved the problem.

Most of the time, however, when the person co-constructs a solution with the therapist, this serves as a

first, albeit significant, step towards problem resolution. I
have shown this in Figure 1.2.

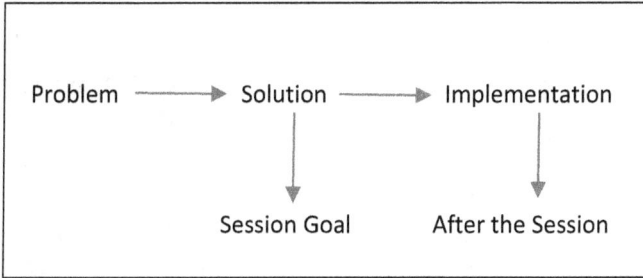

Figure 1.2 Problem, solution and implementation

Thus, I see a single session as the beginning of a
process, rather than the end of the process and I see this
first step towards desired change is beautiful, no matter
how small it may be.

I Invite the Person to Summarise the Session

After the person has come up with a solution, has some
plan for how to implement it and has dealt with potential
obstacles to implementation; then, in my mind, this
signifies that we are approaching the end of the session.
The first thing I do in the ending phase is to ask the person
to summarise the conversation they have had with me. I
do this to gauge what they have found important in the
session. If I summarise the session for them, I am
revealing what I think they have found important in the
session, which may be very different.

I Encourage the Person to Specify Takeaway(s)

Therapy takeaways are learning points that the person has gleaned from the session that have the potential to be implemented through action. These takeaways will likely include the solution discussed in the session (in solution-focused work), but will not be restricted to that. When I elicit takeaways from people, I usually make an effort to encourage them to concentrate on one or two key takeaways alongside the solution and perhaps to consider implementing one (once again, in addition to the solution). The more the individual strives to take away from the session, the less they are likely to do so. Here, as in other single-session work, 'more is less'.

I Encourage the Person to Generalise Their Learning, Whenever Possible

In general, people do not spontaneously generalise their learning across problem-related situations or across problems and need active help to do so. Thus, if there is time and the person is not already overloaded. I will ask if they can see ways of generalising what they are taking away from the session and spend a little time helping them to do so.

Most Often, the Session Initiates Change, Which the Person Develops Outside the Session

I made the point in the section entitled 'Small May Be Beautiful' above that, apart from making a frame change, the person will need to put into practice what they have learned from the session after the session has finished. This is also implied by the development of the action plan and the fact that in order to judge the full impact of the session, the person needs to implement the solution which they developed in the session. The more I can help the person understand that they are responsible for doing this, the more likely they are to do so and the greater the benefit they will derive from the session.

I End the Session Well So that the Person Leaves the Session with Their Morale Restored

Jerome Frank (1961) argued that while people come to psychotherapy with a wide range of symptoms, what is often common in this group is that they come in a state of demoralisation. The task of the therapist, then is to help them restore their morale by the end of therapy. When I conduct the sessions to be discussed in the book, I am guided by the principle in the sense that I want to end the session well so that armed with the learning points and the solution that they derived from the session, the person can be hopeful about their future with respect to addressing the issue for which they sought help.

Ending the session well means giving the person a final opportunity to ask me any questions or telling me anything related to the issue that they may regret not asking me or telling me after the session has finished. This is not an invitation for them to begin discussing a different issue and this should be made quite clear to them when giving them this final opportunity.

I Take Nothing for Granted

People working in SST have noted that they are often surprised by clients. Some clients who they think have got nothing from the session later report significant change and others who they think have learned a lot from the session report no change. Given this, I take nothing for granted and am focused on helping the person with their session goal to the very end of the session. Other less experienced SST therapists may become discouraged midway into the session because of what a client has gone through in the past, for example and tend to think that the person needs more help without giving their all in the current session. I resolutely don't come to any such conclusions because I never know how much such a client is going to benefit from SST until later.

*

This introductory chapter has provided the foundation for the work that I will now present in rest of the book. Let me say a little about the context and process of these sessions.

- Volunteers signed up for a complimentary session of SST with me in response to an invitation from Onlinevents.
- Volunteers signed a contract on which they gave their agreement that the transcript of our session would appear in a book on SST and helping people to get unstuck published by Onlinevents Publications.
- They agreed to provide a follow-up questionnaire a few months after the session.
- They would receive an audio of the recording of the session and a written transcript of the session.
- They had the opportunity of changing their name and other identifiable details.
- They had the opportunity to change their mind about having the session published in the book up to a specified date.

- They would receive a copy of the book on publication.
- Each person was sent a pre-session form, the purpose of which was to help them prepare for the session so that they could get the most from it. I suggested that they returned this to me so that I could get a sense of what they were thinking re the issue.
- Finally, each person was sent a follow-up questionnaire to complete and return so that could gauge what they made of the session.

2

Dealing with Criticism

Date: 10-10-24
Time: 45 mins 16 secs

Sarah Louise's Pre-Session Form

Sarah Louise said that she wanted to focus on the deep pain she experiences when she is criticised and work out why it hurts when she is criticised by some people and not others.

Her *goal* was to get an understanding of the issue and a way of challenging her response to it so that she could feel lighter and happier.

Sarah Louise said that she was not sure that she targeted the issue of criticism even though she has had a lot of therapy on her childhood. She said that she was looking forward to working though the issue of criticism from a different perspective

Sarah Louise listed her inner resources as her past therapy sessions that changed her life, her confidence in her ability to make good of negative experiences and her resilience.

With respect to the help, she wanted to get from the session, Sarah Louise listed: 'Help me solve an emotional or behavioural problem; help me get unstuck.'

The Session

Windy: OK, Sarah Louise, from your perspective what's the purpose of our conversation today?

[This is my typical opening questions in these sessions. I want to ensure that the person and I are on the same page. Once in a similar project, a volunteer came online and in response to this question, said that she wanted supervision on one of her cases related to the subject of the book. We did not proceed.]

Sarah Louise: Well, I'm just looking to explore why I feel triggered by being criticised, to really get underneath that and understand it. And, hopefully, with that understanding, get some new ways of dealing with it, because it's not helpful and I don't want to feel the emotional turmoil of that.

Windy: What is the emotion that you experience?

[While Sarah Louise selected adversity is criticism, a fuller understanding of what she may be stuck with this issue requires me to understand her predominant emotion(s).]

Sarah Louise: The emotion I experience is anxiety ... fear.... [*Pause*] I suppose there's something to do with it linked to a threat of loss: if I'm criticised, does that mean that people won't ... like me? And where does that go?

Windy: OK. So, what would you hope to achieve by the end of our conversation? Is there anything more concrete than that, that you'd like to take away?

     [*Here I am asking for Sarah Louise's session goal.*]

Sarah Louise: ... I just wanna be able to, if someone criticises me, not feel as upset by it. Like some people can just hear something and it's like a water off a duck's back; they don't internalise it and overthink it and try to make sense of it and question their self. I just wanna feel like, 'Oh, it is what it is.' Either accept it's a valid point – it might be something true that they're saying, and then I can work on that if that's something detrimental to me as a person; or it's just their opinion and get over it.

Windy: So, for me, criticism is an adversity, and an adversity is something that happens that's bad. If we said to you, 'Would you like to be criticised or win the lottery?' I guess there's no comparison there. Is there any space to feel healthily bad when you're criticised?

[*My question is based on the position taken by the theory of Rational Emotive Behaviour Therapy (REBT) regarding the distinction between healthy and unhealthy negative emotions. Here, the term 'negative' refers to the feeling tone of the emotion. A healthy negative emotion feels unpleasant but has mostly constructive effects, whereas an unhealthy negative emotion feels unpleasant and has mostly unconstructive effects.*]

Sarah Louise: … Healthily bad? That's a good question. … I suppose, if I understand what you mean by that, could it be a benefit? Could it be a healthy thing to hear?

Windy: But it feels bad. It's something which is negative.

Sarah Louise: Yeah.

Windy: Without the fear. Like it's recognising that you still don't like it but there's no fear attached.

Sarah Louise: Yeah, that's it, isn't it? It's the emotion and the logic. I've got to let go of that fear.

Windy: Well, we'll have a look at that. Do you have this response to everybody who criticises you?

Sarah Louise: No, and this is the thing. This is why I really wanted your help with this because … I'm just trying to think of different scenarios, different individuals, and I feel like, because I've got such a small family, my friends are my family, my chosen family, and I feel like my beliefs are, without my friends, I'm screwed. Without that support system, I'm totally alone. So, I suppose, if they see me in any way that potentially might make me less valuable, then that's a threat to me. So, I don't want to be criticised. That is a particular area of upset for me.

          [*Sarah Louise's response indicates that the focus of our discussion needs to be on being criticised by her friends.*]

Windy: Less valuable to whom?

Sarah Louise: To my friends. My friends are the main people I get triggered by.

Windy: Any friend in particular?

Sarah Louise: Well, an example, this is how crazy this example is, so one of my best friends, I am a godparent to her child – we had to swap chairs at dinner and she went, 'Oh, I haven't got to sit with you, have I?' Now, I don't know if that's criticism, but I took it as. She's mucking about but is there any substance under that? So, I start thinking, 'Well, why wouldn't she want to sit with me? Because my other friend was there and she's more fun, and you wanna be up that end of the table with her, and now you're stuck down here with me.' But then I have this argument, 'Well, you wouldn't ask me to be the godparent of your child if I didn't have a special relationship with you,' but then I thought, 'Maybe I'm not fun. Maybe I'm a secure person, that's why she asked me. But, as a fun friend, I don't bring that attribute, and that's really crap because I wanna be the fun friend as well. I don't just wanna be this secure, safe person for you.' And my other friend, I know she probably does see as more fun. So, I then internalise it.

Windy: So, it sounds like you were having a lot of conversations with her which she didn't play a part in.

Sarah Louise: She had nothing to do with it.

Windy: So, did you ask her what she meant by that?

Sarah Louise: No, because this is where it gets sticky for me and it gets difficult. I then think, 'cos I've got this thing about victim mentality – I can't be the victim. I've done a lot of work to not be a victim of my experiences, and this is why I feel being affected by criticism does upset me because I don't wanna fall in that, 'Oh, why don't you like me?' So, I don't say anything because then it would be me making a big deal out of something, and she'd be like, 'I'm only mucking about.' So, I said, 'Come on, swap with my mate,' and I just tried to make light of it because I don't want to fall into that 'woe is me'.

Windy: Yeah, you don't want to feel a victim and feel sorry for yourself.

Sarah Louise: Yeah, I hate that. That's a big issue. So I then don't want to say these things. But it does upset me. Why don't you want to sit with me? You wouldn't just say that for no reason. That's what my brain tells me.

Windy: And, so that's what you call criticism: there's the implied criticism. How would you take that? You're not fun? You were saying about fun.

Sarah Louise: Yeah, 'I'm not fun. You don't want to spend time with me.'

Windy: You mentioned earlier that without your friends you'd be screwed. Meaning what?

Sarah Louise: I would just feel so alone without my friends. I don't feel I've got an anchor in life. I feel like my anchors are my friends. They're my consistent. They're my safety. They're my support because I don't have that family network. And, like I said before in the email, my partner, he struggles to meet some of the needs within me, so I don't feel like I've got very much of a secure base anywhere.

Windy: Right. What about within yourself?

Sarah Louise: I've been working on it, but I can't shake that feeling of... I'm on my own. So, I do value those friendships.

Windy: Well, 'I'm on my own,' means what to you?

Sarah Louise: ... [*Long pause*] Well, it's just weird. Just lonely and just totally isolated. Scared. Abandoned.

Windy: So, you don't have an idea about yourself that you could be alone but not lonely, alone but still connected.

[*Here, I am working to understand Sarah Louise on the place of friendships in her life and without them she will be, as she says, 'screwed'. In my last question, I am seeing if there is a place in her mind where she can be alone, but not 'screwed', as she put it earlier.*]

Sarah Louise: No, not really.

Windy: The idea that you could, if you were to ever lose your friends, you could make new friends.

Sarah Louise: I have the ability to do that, but I think new friends versus the friends that I'm talking about, it's really hard to get that level of depth.

Windy: Yeah, that's right, but I'm saying, if you had this idea, 'cos it sounds like for you being on your own is a very frightening and negative experience.

Sarah Louise: It is, and I can spend time with myself happily, I quite like my own space at times, but if, it was like I'm alone, I haven't got any friends or me and my partner do split up or something–

Windy: But if that happens, do you have a vision of you rebuilding your life?

Sarah Louise: ... I know eventually I could, but it doesn't feel like a clear, confident thought process. Like some people are like, 'Well, I'd get over it.'

Windy: But why don't you allow it to be unclear and unconfident?

Sarah Louise: It's, I suppose, the discomfort of sitting with that.

Windy: That's right. And what happens when you sit with discomfort?

Sarah Louise: I feel anxious.

Windy: And then?

Sarah Louise: And then I feel sad.

Windy: And then?

Sarah Louise: … [*Pause*] And then I have to get over it.

Windy: Right. So, in other words, eventually you recover.

Sarah Louise: Basically, yeah.

Windy: Is that what happens to you? Do you say, 'Well, look, OK, if the worst comes to the worst and this person is gonna reject me or criticise me,' because it sounds like, if you knew, for example, that your friend was criticising you but they weren't gonna leave you, would that make a difference to you?

Sarah Louise: I don't know because I feel like as well it's so tied up in my personality, like, if you're gonna criticise me, that's a direct attack on me as a person. So, it still would hurt even if I had the reassurance that they would still be there. It's so difficult. It's such a difficult thing.

Windy: Have you got any notepaper?

Sarah Louise: I can write on this.

Windy: Let me see if I can show you something here. Can you see this?

Sarah Louise: Yeah, 'I'.

Windy: Right, OK. So could you do that?

Sarah Louise: Yep. Right, done it.

Windy: What do you see?

Sarah Louise: Loads of little lines?

Windy: What letter are they?

Sarah Louise: 'i'.

Windy: So we've got the big 'I' and the little 'i'.
                    You just do that.

Sarah Louise: I love an exercise like this. This is my
                    thing. OK, I'm doing all the little 'i's
                    inside.

Windy: Now, do you wanna hear my take on
                    something?

Sarah Louise: Yeah, course.

Windy: So, when you're criticised, in reality
                    someone is criticising the small 'i'. You
                    take it as they're criticising the big 'I'.

Sarah Louise: Yeah.

Windy: What would it be if you recognised that,
                    yeah, if your friend criticises you, your
                    initial reflection might be, 'They're
                    criticising all of me,' and then say, 'No,
                    wait a minute, if they are criticising at all,
                    they're only criticising a part of me. And I
                    can either join in the criticism by
                    acknowledging that they may have a point
                    about the small 'i' or I can criticise the
                    whole of me; I could criticise the big 'I'.'

Sarah Louise: Yeah.

Windy: Now, what do you think would happen if
                    you implemented something like that?

Sarah Louise: Well, it definitely helps shift my perspective.

Windy: Right. From what to what?

Sarah Louise: Well, it doesn't feel as heavy. It feels like a smaller rupture.

Windy: Yeah, exactly. The first strand is the idea that, 'If I'm criticised, they're gonna leave me. I'll be all on my own and that's it. I'm screwed.' And I'm saying, if that happens, then, yeah, that would be quite unpleasant, but do you have resources within you that you could bring to the table?

Sarah Louise: I do have resources that I've built up over time and I know I've tapped into when needed. I am a resilient person and I am used to being on my own, believe it or not. I haven't got, like I said, this anchor. People have a mum or a dad or a safe person that will always be there unconditionally. I don't have that.

Windy: Yes you do, and I'm looking at her.

Sarah Louise: Me.

Windy: To paraphrase Michael Jackson, I'm looking at the woman in the mirror, or you could look at the woman in the mirror. So, in a way, it's a different experience of being on your own and being on your own in a way that you could provide your own support. You're not screwed. You're down but you're not out. You're down, you can get up, if it happens. And I think this is where the idea is, because you've got this idea that, 'Anybody that criticises, they're criticising the big 'I' and, since they're criticising the big 'I', they're gonna leave me and, if they left me, I'm screwed.' So what I'm saying is, if the worst comes to the worst and they left you, are you screwed or are you down but not out? And, also, when they criticise you, are they criticising the big 'I' or are they criticising the small 'i'?

[In this part of the session, I am helping Sarah Louise to make a number of points: (i) If Sarah Louise does lose her friends she can build a new set of friends eventually and her resilience will help her to do that; (ii) if a friend criticises her, they are probably criticising one of her little i's and not her Big I. Even if they do criticise her Big I she can choose to join in with such criticism or not; (iii) Sarah Louise can accept that her first reaction may be a disturbed one, but she can stand back and respond constructively to that first response. It would have better if I

*had separated these points out and had
Sarah Louise consider them one by one.*]

Sarah Louise: Yeah. That's a very, very good way of
reframing it.

Windy: Now, the other thing you mentioned, and
I think that one of the things that's gonna
stop you from dealing with it is the idea
that, 'If I raise it with them, I'm being a
victim. I can't say anything because I'll
be a victim.'

[*I am framing this issue as an obstacle to
discussing it with her friends. It would
have been better if I had asked Sarah
Louise how she saw it and whether she
wanted to discuss it. I also wonder if I am
covering too much ground in this
session.*]

Sarah Louise: Yeah.

Windy: Now, the question is, is it possible for you
to say something without being a victim?

Sarah Louise: I suppose that particular friend I would
say no. I have said things in the past to her
and I've held her accountable for stuff
that's upset me, and she was quite took
aback. She was totally blindsided by it,
but she did appreciate it and there was a

change. So that's fine. But she's a very, very defensive person.

Windy: Right. I guess your options are, if she's a defensive person, 'therefore, I'm not gonna say anything,' or she's a defensive person, 'so I'm gonna have to go very carefully here.'

Sarah Louise: Yeah. It's hard. I think where my brain goes with this is I show up in a lot of ways for my friends and I don't always get that back, and it's hard because where obviously I put a lot of energy into that, the output versus what I get back isn't always matched.

Windy: Yeah, but look what happens in the way you try to deal with the mismatch. How do you try to deal with the mismatch?

Sarah Louise: … I try not to give as much any more.

Windy: Right, and do they notice?

Sarah Louise: … Well, an example is, when I had my son who's two, I'm one of the last people to have a kid in my group 'cos we're older mums, but they had kids a bit before me, and, because I don't now have that extra time, I have had to give less, and they have noticed but I find the relationships haven't been as held onto. It's not like that deficit's been made up by them. It's just gone less. Do you know what I mean?

Windy: Yeah. And what do you want from them?

Sarah Louise: ... I suppose just equality.

Windy: And how are you gonna get it?

Sarah Louise: ... By matching them.

Windy: It's interesting, some of the time when I'm working with counsellors, with clients, I have to say to them, 'Wait a minute, there's something you're neglecting here,' and they say, 'What?' and I say, 'You can talk to them about it.'

Sarah Louise: Yeah.

Windy: And you're reluctant to do that.

Sarah Louise: Not all of them. Only certain ones.

Windy: Right, but if you see the value of being able to at least address things with certain people that you can and with others you may have to go carefully, like your highly defensive friend, but it is still possible that you can talk about it with them, but you may have to take care with some people and less care with others. But it's almost like your thing is that you match them and, therefore, you withdraw. Part of you hopes that they'll say, 'Oh, you've withdrawn. What's wrong?' but they don't. They may withdraw because they may have the same idea. And then where are you?

Sarah Louise: Yeah, exactly. I find, though, because of this era that I'm in, everyone's so busy with young children. It's crazy. I literally couldn't have imagined how much having a child impacts your time, your priorities. And I think everyone's in that stage where they've got such small capacity to be a mum, to do a job, to give their time to their partner. And I think my issue is, because I'm not really connected in my relationship, I've probably got a bit more capacity to wanna do stuff, whereas their priority's their direct, immediate family, and I don't even have that. So, I think, for me, I need to fill my cup elsewhere or try to, like you said, come back to myself, be my own anchor, because they're not doing anything wrong.

Windy: No.

Sarah Louise: It's not that they don't care about me. And I know that logically it's just the emotional of just, 'Oh, where is everyone when they know I need 'em?' and then I fall into the victim, and then I hate it. So there's this cycle.

Windy: Yeah, exactly. But it's almost as if you see the idea of sadness, 'I'm sad because I'm not connected with them,' you put it under the heading of 'victim' and that's the bit that you hate and, therefore, you throw the baby out of the bathwater because there's still the sadness but, because you actually put the 'poor me' to it, whereas I'm saying you could take 'poor me' out of it, but you're still sad 'cos you're not connected as you'd like to be, and you could tell them, 'I miss you. I know we're all busy but I'm wondering if I could see you or talk to you?' or something like that. But you don't allow yourself to do that because you've got, 'I'm a victim. I don't allow myself to be a victim.' It sounds to me that you can actually allow yourself to feel sad without being a victim.

Sarah Louise: Yeah. I need to detach the two. I suppose I just hate being thought of as this.

Windy: Sure. I mean, I hate being thought of as an old bald geyser, but, if you allow people to think about you – well, in my case it is, but in your case, if they think you're a victim, does that make you a victim?

Sarah Louise: I don't know. I suppose, coming back to this criticism, if they're thinking, 'Oh, she's such a victim,' is there any truth in it? I'm always questioning is it a projection from their stuff or is it that's generally the case? And I don't wanna be that, so I've got to look at that. I've got to do an internal enquiry about that.

Windy: Yeah, sure, but I think that's always a good thing to do because you've got that tendency to confuse the big 'I' and the little 'i'. They might say you're a victim but, in reality, if you are a victim, you're only a victim in that small area of your life. It doesn't make the whole of you a victim. But in may not mean that you're a victim at all and they may have you wrong.

Sarah Louise: … I'm drawn to these people. I've got a handful of people, I emailed you some of the people, so you know they're my people, I love them so much, but then I'm drawn to other people that are, I just feel like, emotionally unavailable. I am more in than them. That's how it feels, anyway. But then I look at it and I'm really questioning is that true.

Windy: Well, when you say you're drawn to it, you mean it's familiar to you or what?

Sarah Louise: Well, take for instance, my mum, who's passed now, but she was very emotionally unavailable and very critical. My dad literally has got no sociability at all. He doesn't talk, doesn't have many friends, very introverted, doesn't really speak to me. So, I've got these two caregivers, they're just not there. And then my partner, very emotionally unavailable, non-committal even though we've been together many, many years. And then even my best friend, she's very logical, she's not emotional. Although she's my secure person, it's still you give her a hug, she's got her arms by her side. And the defensive friend, everyone wants to be her friend, and I'm like, 'I should be your priority 'cos I'm one of your best friends.' I'm always trying to get more than what people are willing to give me. I'm choosing that for a reason. Is that because that's what I'm used to? And then they're the sort of people that would be critical.

Windy: Well, there are two things here. The question is, 'Am I drawn to people who are unavailable because that's the prototype that I'm used to. I'm used to that with my mum, I'm used to that with my dad. And, therefore, maybe that's familiar to me and that's it.' But the other thing that I'm hearing is the idea of, 'You're my best friend and I should be your best friend, so I should be your priority,' which is a different take on that, isn't it? I can't see the connection there quite easily. Are they the opposite side of the same coin or are they different? I'm not sure,

[*Having worked in a more connected and collaborative way on the 'If they criticise me I'll end up being screwed and the 'Big-I-little I' I'm screwed, when we discuss the 'victim issue, I am struggling to find a workable focus. Instead. I'm covering too much ground.*]

Sarah Louise: I don't know. I don't know if I'm just setting myself up to fail by wanting something from people that they just don't have the ability to give.

Windy: Is there any problem with wanting it? The question is, after wanting it you could ask yourself, 'Do I want it and, therefore, I've gotta have it?' or, 'Do I want it because it's important to me, but I also recognise that I don't have to have it?' Which way are you gonna take your wants? Are you gonna convert it into something which is necessary for you or are you gonna leave it as a want with the conversion?

Sarah Louise: Yeah. It comes back to, you know when you talk to somebody about getting into a relationship and they say, 'I always pick the red flags, and I don't realise they're red flags, and then I'm in too deep by the time I realise and then I'm gonna get hurt.' And it's really difficult. I suppose, we're coming back to the friendships, relationships are one thing, but friendships I just find so much more painful to be. I don't know why. Friendships seem to hurt more. Friendships I can't let go of.

Windy: Do you have any friends you do want to let go of?

Sarah Louise: I have some friends that over time I've very much distanced myself from They've hurt me and disrespected me many years ago, and I thought, 'What value are you bringing to me?' So, I thought, 'No. Apart from you shitting on me, basically, you're not bringing too much else to the table,' therefore they're easier to distance from. So, they're already gone, not fully but mostly. But, yeah, I struggle with endings. I struggle with letting go. I stay in things longer than I should.

Windy: Right, but is there anybody that you're with at the moment that you are staying in longer than you believe is good for you?

Sarah Louise: Well, I suppose my actual long-term partner. It's hard for me to actually say that.

Windy: Alright. Before we get into that, can we get some closure on the other issue in terms of the criticism? So maybe you wanna review what we've done so far on that thing about criticism first?

[*I wish I had done this before going with the 'victim' issue which really didn't go anywhere.*]

Sarah Louise: Yeah. Well, I suppose it's just making sense of, when I hear somebody say something that I interpret as criticism, I need to recognise that it's not me, it's just a part of me, a small 'i' which helps buffer that pain. That's what I need to take forward in my mind.

Windy: What about the idea that, if it was big 'I' and they did leave you, how are you gonna deal with that?

Sarah Louise: I'd be anxious and sad, and then I'd get over it. I'd have to get over it.

Windy: Right.

Sarah Louise: The world will still keep turning.

Windy: Yeah, and that experience, as I often say, is a part of the world, not the end of the world.

Sarah Louise: Yeah.

Windy: So, do you think you'll be able to utilise those two ideas going forward?

Sarah Louise: Yeah. It's a really good thing to think about, to keep me safe psychologically from absorbing it all.

Windy: And what about the idea that, 'I can't really say anything because that's me feeling sorry for myself and me being a victim'?

Sarah Louise: Yeah, I still am struggling with not wanting to come across that way, but I'm not scared of having uncomfortable conversations. I do feel I have the ability to talk about things in the right way that wouldn't land wrong. I feel like it's one of them pick your battles: is it something that I really need to say?

Windy: Which battle?

Sarah Louise: You know they say pick your battles? So, I think, before I go in, do I need to say anything? I need to be able to work out,

'Is this my stuff or does this generally need to be addressed?'

Windy: Sure. That's a good question. But I'm saying, if you conclude that it does need to be addressed and you address it and they see you as being a victim, are they right or are they wrong?

Sarah Louise: No, they're wrong.

Windy: That's right. So, if you allow people to be wrong, even a best friend can be wrong, because they're bringing their own sort of viewpoint, it sounds like to me.

Sarah Louise: Yeah.

Windy: 'Cos at the moment it sounds like you're ruling any kind of conversation out because you see it as playing the victim and you fear that other people see you as playing the victim. And that's something that, 'In no way, shape or form do I want anybody to see me as a victim.' But they still might.

Sarah Louise: Yeah.

Windy: And, since you don't have any control over their minds, you've only got control how you deal with that, you could actually ask yourself, 'Well, I don't like them thinking about that but are they right or are they wrong?'

Sarah Louise: Yeah.

Windy: And, even if you are a victim, are you a big 'I' victim or little 'i' victim?

Sarah Louise: Yeah. I know I'm not a big 'I' victim because I am a go-getter. I can do this. I've got that power and resilience and motivation in many ways. In other ways I do feel powerless. So, I suppose it's that conflicted stuff within me.

Windy: Yeah. I mean, it's about you developing a more complex view of yourself as somebody who's largely not a victim but being a human being you're not immune. You weren't immunised against victimhood at some point, were you? Give you an injection. Come here for your mumps, your rubella and your anti-victim jab.

Sarah Louise: I'd like that if they'd done that.

Windy: I know, but they didn't have that.

Sarah Louise: That will be in the future.

Windy: They still don't. But you take my point.

Sarah Louise: Yeah, I do.

Windy: What's my point?

Sarah Louise: That I'm not a victim. There might be a part of me that could feel victimised, but that's not me as a whole.

> [*At least, Sarah Louise is going to take away something constructive from our discussion on the victim issue.*]

Windy: Yeah, exactly. So I think, if you can really recognise that that's where your power is – your power is in how you choose to define yourself, given a standing back view of what's going on and that you can choose, therefore, to assert yourself and speak your mind should you choose to, taking due care and intention about who you're talking to. But it sounds like you have been reluctant to have those conversations with friends.

Sarah Louise: Yeah. I think I need to have a sit down and have a think about it, who I would like to talk to and how I can resolve some of this stuff.... 'Cos, like I said, some people it is what it is, but others there is opportunities I think to have a chat.

Windy: Yeah. And you'll know these people quite well. You'll know what's best. But just to say, 'Look, I miss you. It would be nice to see more of you.' I can't see anybody rejecting you as a result of saying that.

Sarah Louise: Yeah.

Windy: If they do, one has to wonder about what kinds of friends they are.

Sarah Louise: Well, yeah, exactly. Yeah, they're not gonna reject me on that.

Windy: Yeah. The bit about letting go of people, what's that about?

Sarah Louise: I don't know. I find it irritating.... I really do.... I don't know.... [*Pause*] I suppose I'm like who I would actually wanna let go of. Do I? I don't think I do. If I did, why do I struggle?

Windy: Yeah, you mentioned your partner.

[*This is an error. I have already covered too much ground and in doing so, I have violated the more is less principle that is a foundation of SST.*]

Sarah Louise: Oh yeah. Yeah, we've just been trying for so long to make it work and it just doesn't work. And I know that and it just hurts to actually say it out loud.

Windy: Have you had couples' counselling?

Sarah Louise: Yep.

Windy: That didn't go anywhere?

Sarah Louise: It did pre-baby. We had some real good direction and structure. I think the other side of having the baby, just so much pressure, sleep deprivation, financial pressure and everything else. Our capacity to reconcile has gone. We just can't come back together. We just blow up, blow up, blow up, and then there's just no resolve, really. It's like the cycle. It's like we're stuck. And I think the therapist we were seeing, I feel like she checked out, and that was really hard 'cos she wasn't even interrupting us. And I was like, 'I could've had this row at home.' I think I really did have it at home. It was quite difficult. He's avoidant, I'm anxious. He withdraws, I'm constantly wanting that reassurance. And I'm affectionate, he's not.

Windy: Reassurance for what?

Sarah Louise: Well, just wanting to feel connected. Wanting to feel valuable. And he's very independent. So, it's hard for him to lean on me. Whereas I'm a giver. So, it's like I would love him to take me up on that, and he doesn't. So, there's a lot of needs that don't get met and then I get upset or whatever and he's like, 'You're not being very nice.' And I'm like, 'But I am being nice, but you just don't wanna take it.' So, we get into a cycle. But, yeah, we have a lot of issues since having our baby and that's just really reaffirmed we just don't work.

Windy: And that sounds like it falls outside of the idea of criticism, dealing with criticism, doesn't it?

[*At least, I point this out.*]

Sarah Louise: Well, yeah. I was thinking about how it's relevant, and he does criticise me, but he says I'm the critical one. I'm not blindsided by that. I know I can say stuff that seems critical, but I think at the core we always say what is it – the chicken or the egg that comes first? Is it because he's doing something, I then criticise or am I criticising so then he's withdrawing? And I often do find it's because he's so independent, I'm just always left on me own again.

Windy: Right. So, if you were to do one thing differently that might help to turn things around since he's not here, for me to ask that same question, what would that one thing be?

Sarah Louise: It would probably be to just suck it up and be my truth, authentic, kind, funny, loving self in the hope that that would bring him out of his protective bubble.

Windy: Right. How long are you prepared to do that experiment for?

Sarah Louise: Well, I did once try it for three days and I got nothing, so I thought, 'Bollocks to this.'

Windy: Well, do you think three days to change a pattern like that is gonna be enough?

Sarah Louise: It wasn't but I was think, 'God, give me something.' He internalises stuff and holds onto it a lot longer. I can be quite explosive and I'll get over it in a matter of minutes. He'll hear that.

Windy: What if you gave it two weeks, not three days?

Sarah Louise: OK. So I'm gonna tell you I will make a commitment, 'cos I love accountability. I love to have someone to hold me accountable, it really helps. So, I will do that for two weeks. What I found in the past is, when I change and I'm nice, whatever, he will still find something to criticise me about.

Windy: Well, we don't know yet.

Sarah Louise: Well, no, I have tried.

Windy: Three days.

Sarah Louise: No, but there's been other times. So, basically, I'll do stuff like I'm kind, I'm doing this, this, this and this and then I'm going over and above to make sure he doesn't hear me in a critical way, and then he's like, 'Stop being passive-aggressive.' And I'm like, 'Oh my God, I'm generally not. I'm trying everything I can.' So, if I'm outward aggressive, he's moaning about it and, if I'm kind, he says I'm being passive. And I generally would be telling you if I had been.

Windy: So, what response would he see in you that he would value?

Sarah Louise: … It's really hard because he wants to be the good guy. So, if I ever fall into the category I'm the good one, he clings onto that label. He doesn't wanna ever be the one that's to blame. So, it's really hard for me to step into that. So, yeah, I think I've just gotta keep going with it and see what happens. Keep being kind. Keep being light-hearted. Not react. Don't react to him, is what I've got to do.

Windy: Yeah, and you'll see what comes back, 'cos, if you give something, a decent crack of the whip, sometimes the changes will occur a little bit later because the person might not even see the change. So that might be a useful thing to do. And it sounds like you're not taking the criticism from him as badly as you do from your friends anyway.

Sarah Louise: I don't know why, and this is why I'm trying to work it out. When he criticises me, I don't know.

Windy: Do you think he's gonna leave you?

Sarah Louise: Well, we have kind of spoke about separating. But it's been going on so long, I don't know if I've been grieving it slowly.

Windy: But does the thought of him leaving you and your friends leaving you, is that a different kind of fear?

Sarah Louise: Yeah.

Windy: In what way?

Sarah Louise: It's so weird. I suppose with my friends I just see them safer.

Windy: And, if you were to lose the safety, that sounds like it's a different type of loss.

Sarah Louise: I don't feel like I'm prioritised by him. So, an example, something really good happened in my life – in more recent years I will tell my friends, I won't really bother telling him. He doesn't seem as interested. So, it's like they, obviously, on some level hold more value for me.

Windy: Yeah, and maybe that means that the threat is less of loss because they're less valuable. Obviously, it's kind of difficult to deal with a couple situation, but at least you've got something to see what happens if you stick to it for a longer period of time.

We're approaching the end, so let's see what you're gonna take away from this that you're gonna implement, Sarah Louise . What are you gonna implement?

[*I manage to suggest something of value concerning her partner, but I still think it would have been better not to go with this issue. We could have spent the time more productively developing an action plan with respect to how she could deal with criticism, for example.*]

Sarah Louise: Well, we spoke about the 'I'. We spoke about me having difficult conversations. I think I just wanna be more thick-skinned and not just absorb everything as a threat response. I'm so quick to get into that fight or flight, I don't wanna abandon myself to then appease other people so that they don't criticise me.

Windy: And what I'm saying there is, if you can really turn to yourself as your own safety resource; you don't put all the safety into the friends basket. You put it into the Sarah Louise basket.

Sarah Louise: Yeah, 'cos, thinking about it, they've all got their flaws. There's a load of things I could be critical of them. It's not like they're perfect and I'm this flawed person.

Windy: No.

Sarah Louise: I need to remember that when I'm feeling emotionally charged and upset.

Windy: Yeah. In a sense, you know those little 'i's in the big 'I' – some of them are positive, some of them are negative, some of them are neutral. And that applies to you and to them. And you know what we call somebody with good points, negative points and neutral points?

Sarah Louise: No.

Windy: What do you think we call them?

Sarah Louise: Well, I'd say whole authentic person.

Windy: Human.

Sarah Louise: Human.

Windy: You're human, they're human. And people who are defensive are threatened by the idea that, 'If I own up to something negative, it makes the whole of me negative and then I'll be left.' So, I think, if you hold onto that idea, that would be really good.

Sarah Louise: That's really helpful. I'm writing that down. … [*Pause*] Yeah, that's really, really helpful. Thank you, Windy. I've really enjoyed our session. I really appreciate being a part of the book and everything.

Windy: OK. As I say, I'll send you the recording. It will come from something called pCloud, so just be mindful of that. And then the transcript will come later.

Sarah Louise: Lovely. When do you expect to publish the book and everything?

Windy: About a year's time.

Sarah Louise: Thank you so much.

Sarah Louise's Follow-Up Questionnaire

Date: 11-12-24

Question	Response
1. What progress did you make on the issue that you brought to the session. Indicate the amount of progress you have made on this issue by using a 0% (no progress) – 100% (problem solved) scale.	**Issue Brought to the Session (Please name this):** Feeling criticised by a friend **Amount of progress made:** 70% **Factors that helped me make progress:** Thinking of how feeling criticised doesn't have to evoke a strong emotional response. If it is true then it's only a criticism of a part of me and it doesn't have to be all consuming. **Factors that were absent that could have helped me make more progress:** Perhaps more around projection, am I critical of others?

2. Did you make any progress on other issues that you have that you did not bring to our session? Please elaborate.	Yes, I have used the big I little I technique to apply to other interactions where I previously may have felt attacked, I now have the awareness to see this as a much lesser problem
3. How would you describe your relationship with Windy Dryden in the session?	Windy created a welcoming and safe space, I felt he asked the right questions to build a picture and explore why I was reacting with fear of rejection when experiencing criticism.
4. What, if anything, did Windy Dryden do during the session that was helpful to you?	Challenged my perspective to help me reframe
5. What, if anything, did Windy Dryden do during the session that was unhelpful to you?	N/A

6. How helpful did you find the pre-session form if you were sent one? Please elaborate.	Helpful in the sense I knew what example to bring to session, however, I typically allow for a natural in the moment process when thinking about emotionally charged experiences. Considering it was one session, it definitely prevented wasting time so we could dive straight in.
7. How helpful did you find the audio-recording of your session? Please elaborate.	I haven't listened to this yet as I have a clear enough memory of our session, and have retained the areas important for me to take forward. I think it is valuable to have considering it is one session, as I may look back over it and it would be especially helpful if I'd not had much therapy previously.
8. How helpful did you find the transcript of your sessions? Please elaborate.	I haven't read this yet as I have a clear enough memory of our session, and have retained the areas important for me to take forward. I think it is valuable to have considering it is one session, as I may look back over it and it would be especially helpful if I'd not had much therapy previously.

9. How does Single-Session Therapy compare with other therapies that you have had? Please elaborate.	It is very solution-focused, which is good to feel like you can fully work through a challenge and leave with the tools and awareness to overcome it. Almost instant gratification!
10. What improvements, if any, do you think need to be made to the Single-Session Therapy framework?	Possibly prompts for self-reflection/journaling on said topic to take out into the world as a way of redirecting clients back if they begin to struggle again.
11. Please give any additional feedback that your responses to the questions above have not covered.	Overall a great experience and way of working, highlights the success if focusing strategically on one core issue and working through it.

My Reflections and Summary

Upon reading the transcript of the session, I concluded that I did help Sarah Louise with the issue she had come for help with – understanding her response to criticism and finding a way to deal with it. However, I was disappointed with my behaviour in the session in several respects. First, I did not separate Sarah Louise's two responses to criticism – 'I'm screwed' and 'I'm less valuable' and deal with them one at a time. Although Sarah Louise was able to take something important from this convoluted discussion, this was despite my efforts, not because of them. I also did not address Sarah Louise's issue of being a victim in a clear way, although I was able to apply the 'Big I – little I' concept that Sarah Louise found helpful in our discussion of dealing with criticism to this issue. Finally, I covered too much ground and ideally should not have dealt with the issue of Sarah Louise's relationship with her partner, and, indeed, very little came out of this discussion.

This session shows that a person can gain quite a lot from a single session even when the therapist's contribution is not very skilful. Sarah Louise said on a 0–100% scale she made 70% progress on her nominated issue and applied the Big I-little i technique to other interactions where she previously may have felt attacked, This awareness has helped her to see this as a much lesser problem.

Commenting on our therapeutic relationship, Sarah Louise said that I created a welcoming and safe space and asked the right questions to build a picture and explore why she was reacting with fear of rejection when experiencing criticism. She said that what I did that was most helpful was to challenge her perspective, which led to a frame change solution.

Concerning the pre-session form, the audio recording and the transcript, Sarah Louise said the following:

• She said that the pre-session form was helpful in the sense that she knew what example to bring to the session. She also said that it prevented wasting time so we could dive straight in to her nominated issue.

- She had neither listened to the audio-recording nor read transcript because she had kept in mind what she needed to take forward. She did say, however, that it was good to have both available should she decide to consult them in the future.

The only factor she believed was missing that could have been beneficial was 'perhaps more around projection, am I critical of others?'

3

Dealing with Unrequited Love

Date: 10-10-24
Time: 41 mins 30 secs

Ruth's Pre-Session Form

Ruth mentioned on her pre-session form that she wanted to discuss being in a relationship with emotionally avoidant partners, and her compassionate nature being seen as a weakness.

Her *goal* was to try to understand how this happens and why she walks away after many years. She had suggested couples therapy to her last partner, with whom this had happened, but this was the catalyst for the end of the relationship. Ruth said that her strengths are that she is assertive, strong and compassionate.

The Session

Windy: So, Ruth, from your perspective what's the purpose of our conversation today?

Ruth: I guess it's a one-off session about, I think it was unrequited love, quite a pattern in my life, if you like, of feeling that I'm giving more than I'm getting in a relationship.

Windy: OK. And that is directly happening now?

Ruth: The relationship has just ended. So, three weeks ago, I moved back to my house where my son lives because it was just unbearable.

Windy: So, what would you like to take away from today?

[I ask Ruth about her goals from the session.]

Ruth: I think I'd like to take away someone else's perspective. This isn't things that I talk about to others. People see my worldview very differently and from the beginning of the relationship it was, 'You two are gonna clash. Don't bother,' etc. So, it's about pulling it apart and seeing how I can change my behaviours for the future, or I will remain single.

[Ruth wants a different perspective and to change her behaviours.]

Windy: So, what behaviours do you need to change that, from your perspective, contribute to the problem?

[In retrospect, I could have asked Ruth which of her two goals she would like to pursue first. By asking about one, I am leading the session rather than being client-led.]

Ruth: … I believe what contributes to the problem is choice of partner. I've never made the choice of a partner. They've sort of wooed me, if you like. That's an old-fashioned term, but wooed me. So, I've not really gone out to seek out a partner. And my training and my belief system – I work really hard throughout the years to be compassionate, caring, nonjudgmental, all the bases of therapy, really. And it makes me become very unstuck in relationships when there is conflict.

Windy: It helps you to become unstuck?

Ruth: Yeah. I mean, I used unstuck as… *[pause]*, yeah, there's no sort of mending. I would use the word 'stuck' but there's no stuckness 'cos I can choose to leave at any time. So, for me, my behaviour makes me become… unstuck in a way that I don't really know what I'm adhering to, if that makes sense. I don't know if I'm making any sense.

Windy: You don't know what you're adhering to?

Ruth: Yes.

Windy: What would you like to adhere to?

Ruth: A very loving two-way understanding relationship that's not me doing all the forgiving.

Windy: Right. And, so, when you notice that that isn't happening in a relationship, 'cos it might not, how do you deal with it?

Ruth: I usually wait for change. I don't actively pursue change but I wait for things to settle because people are all different. I can't expect somebody to be very like me because I'm quite feminine in my approach. I can't expect my partner to be as understanding or caring, etc., as me.

Windy: And what has the impact of you waiting for change?

Ruth: Things don't change. Things become worse.

Windy: OK. So, would you say that waiting for change, in the words of Dr Phil: 'How's that working for you?', would you agree that it's not working for you?

Ruth: It's not working for me at all.

Windy: So, what are the options to do something different?

Ruth: I think past history, when I was younger before I got married, if my boyfriends at the time annoyed me, I'd be gone. So, I never gave them a chance. And I guess now I've got older I'm just trying to give someone a chance to settle and not be so directive. And what do I have to change? I guess this is my struggle. I know in my gut that things aren't working but I try and give somebody time to think maybe this will work in the end.

Windy: But how much time are you giving them?

Ruth: This time was five years, so it's a long time.

Windy: If you wanted to take a bus and the bus wasn't coming, how long would you wait for the bus to come?

Ruth: I have done that and I usually wait a good hour or so. I don't walk to get another bus.

Windy: Well, what would you conclude after the hour?

Ruth: That another bus is coming but it may not be en route yet.

Windy: Yeah, or maybe they've changed the route or maybe they've cancelled the route. But you don't wait five years for the bus to come.

Ruth: No, I wouldn't wait five years. That would be quite odd.

Windy: You used to have the idea – it's a shame your name's not Renee because we could sing *Just Walk Away, Renee* – 'So, if they piss me off, I'm off – piss off, off,' type of thing. Now you've gone the other extreme, if you don't mind me saying so, where you're saying, 'Well, I've got to let them settle. Settling is good,' but it sounds like five years, so that's not working. What other options are available to you?

              [*Ruth frames her issue as one where she is chosen by a man who turns out to be emotionally avoidant. Rather than using one of her listed strengths of assertion to address the situation in which her desires for closeness are not being met, she waits for her partner to change. However, they do not, and she continues to wait.*]

Ruth: Gosh. I mean, in this current one I did try everything. I tried to passively talk about what was happening, and in passively I mean very gently so it doesn't come across as an attack. That it's quite a situationship, not a relationship, 'cos there was no companionship. There was nothing, no intimacy. And I would say, 'What is this? Shall we stay together? Should we part because I'm quite miserable and you're quite miserable?' and the answer was that there's no problem. There was never a recognition of problem. So, I tried to passively speak about it to have some sort of resolve. As I say, I did suggest couples' therapy which went down like a lead balloon because they didn't see a problem. And I guess maybe that's what I need to look at. This may be my issue that I have to take ownership of. Like you say, how long do you stay in a situationship where there is no intimacy, there is no love, there's no companionship, there's no shared interest?

Windy: How is that your issue?

Ruth: Because I stayed.

Windy: Oh yeah, that's right. It's not your issue, it sounds to me, if you say, 'It's my issue. I should be able to put up with this,' kind of thing. You're aware that this person is not meeting your important desires. You have tried to address it in a number of ways. Did you end the relationship? Did they end the relationship? How did it end?

Ruth: Do you want the whole story, Windy?

Windy: No, we ain't got time for the whole story.

Ruth: It ended on the Eiffel Tower in Paris.

Windy: What, you pushed him over?

Ruth: I wish I could've. There was an engagement happening. So, me and this chap have got history since the 80s. We had history, a long history. We went to the top of the Eiffel Tower. It's somewhere I always wanted to go. I went to the Moulin Rouge which he absolutely hated. And there were couples celebrating, getting engaged, lots of champagne, and I said, 'That should be us, really,' and he actually said, 'Absolutely not, ever. I can't stand you.' And that was it, really. So, I moved out when we got back. I was just dumbstruck. I think, why take me to Paris for the weekend to do that. It was very bizarre.

Windy: OK. So, you tried to bring about change. Looking back at it, at what point do you think, 'The learning is that after a certain period of time, if I'm not getting what I want, I'm off'?

Ruth: I think the week after I moved in, I should've left.

Windy: How long was that into the relationship?

Ruth: … Two years of sort of dating and I moved in. So, the reason I moved in was, as I say we've got a long history of knowing each other, his mum passed away on my birthday four years ago and I was with him 'cos he was on his own and I went to the hospice to see her and him. And I think his mum actually said to him, 'That's the girl that you should've been with all your life,' etc. So, I think he felt a duty to his mum, maybe. I don't know. I don't understand the dynamics behind it. I'm not him.

Windy: No.

Ruth: I moved in a year after she passed and it was my birthday. My family, we're from a traveller community, they go over the top on a birthday. I had lots of cards and balloons and I put them in the front room and he went ballistic because he said it was an insult to his mother's memory because she died on my birthday. From that day, he was miserable. I put it down to grief, Windy. I thought, 'Well, he's grieving. Give him some space, he's grieving.' But it never got better.

Windy: Let him settle. Give him some space. And your desires, where do they come?

Ruth: … [*Pause*] I had to try and ignore them.

Windy: OK. So, let's see what you can learn from that, then. So, you did make some efforts to improve things in a very gentle way. They didn't work. You let him settle, you gave him some space, you submerged your desires. So, what do you want to change in those aspects?

Ruth: … I mean, to be honest, I shouldn't have stayed. I knew it wasn't working.

Windy: Why did you?

Ruth: I think because I actually felt quite secure and sorry for him because he's very isolated; he doesn't mix with many people.

Windy: Other pity. Right. What are you laughing about?

Ruth: I'm laughing at that word, pity.

Windy: Well, it is, isn't it?

Ruth: Pity and sympathy. And that's not a good basis for a relationship. I mean, I know that I worked.

Windy: So, is that a vulnerability point for you, feeling sorry for somebody?

[*It emerges from our conversation that in the relationship that we are discussing, she submerges her desire for intimacy, waits for*

him to change, which she does not do and
stays partly because she feels secure and
partly because she feels sorry for him.]

Ruth: Absolutely. I've always worked alongside
my practice in drop-in centres, homeless
centres.

Windy: Yeah, but you've never had a relationship
with everybody.

Ruth: No.

Windy: Exactly.

Ruth: I felt like that, Windy. I'm a survivor of
domestic violence many, many years ago and
I was left with nothing. And I had a lot of
therapy over it. It's not a trauma for me.

Windy: And did you feel sorry for yourself?

Ruth: I didn't, no.

Windy: So, you can be all those things and not feel
sorry for yourself, and he can have all these
things and you don't have to pity him. I make
a distinction between pitying a person which
is saying: this person is a poor person, versus
they're a non-poor person but they are in a
poor situation.

Ruth: Yes, because they're very ego-driven, very good job, almost psychopathic, I would say, very driven by money. I'm not at all. Always working. That's their whole life, is earning money and working.

Windy: So far, I can't see what brought you together.

Ruth: That's what everybody says – why?

Windy: What's your answer?

Ruth: I've been looking at it and my father was in the navy and my father was away a lot. So, there's a sort of thing there about somebody emotionally unavailable, I think. This is what I've been thinking about in the last week.

Windy: Well, because it's familiar?

Ruth: Because it's familiar.

Windy: Or, 'Because somehow, if I manage to convert him round, I'll finally convert my father around'? I don't know.

Ruth: I think because, I mean he left me alone. There were demands, which went the other way. So, there were no demands.

Windy: From him.

Ruth: From him there were no demands. It was just, 'Be here, treat the place as your own.' But there was nothing else with that.

Windy: Right. So, he gave you some space and freedom, which is important to you?

Ruth: It's important to me in a way, but there was no companionship.

Windy: No. So, you got certain things but not the most important things which were companionship, a loving relationship, somebody who actually values you. Now, the question is, going forward is that what you want?

Ruth: … I don't want to be in the same situation that I find myself in all the time because I don't put demands on anyone. I don't want to live like that again because it's awful being lonely in a relationship.

Windy: Yeah.

Ruth: And wanting to do things together and the other person has got no interest at all in doing anything. So, I'm always on my own. My friends are all married. They're all married and in couples, and I will say all of them; I don't have any single friends. So, I'm always the odd one out, if you like, although I'm never made to feel that.

Windy: No, but, going forward, would you like a relationship which is based on more that the person is going to offer you some love and affection and want to be with you as well as some freedom?

[As we discuss the story of her recent relationship, it emerges that Ruth wants both freedom and companionship, which we can say taken together may form her goal for a relationship.]

Ruth: Absolutely.

Windy: Right, OK. Now, the question is, are you open to the idea that, if you meet somebody like that and they start not to give those conditions, that you actually address it with them?

Ruth: … Eventually.

Windy: Well, yes, but that's the trouble, isn't it, with you, Ruth – eventually: 'I've got to let them settle.' What's the obstacle for you?

[I pick up on the word 'eventually' here. As it appears that she is afraid of addressing a situation where her desire for closeness is not met.]

Ruth: Conflict. I cannot do conflict at all.

Windy: You're not having conflict. You're having a discussion.

[*I could have asked about this, not declared it.*]

Ruth: I think some people cannot have discussions because they see it as a threat.

Windy: But then you're finding out quickly.

Ruth: Yes.

Windy: The point is, if you have a discussion about this – because you have a fear of conflict, you don't say anything for a long time and, when you say anything, then it's another five years gone. I mean, yes, if you're gonna live to the ripe old age of 650, then I think you're fine; it's a good timetable. But I'm just saying that, if you had the discussion and somebody acts in a really aggressive way towards you or anything like that, what does that tell you?

Ruth: That they are not on my wavelength and they're quite threatened.

Windy: Right, and would you want a relationship with such a person?

Ruth: No.

Windy: So, then you walk away.

Ruth: Yeah.

Windy: So, what I'm saying is it's almost like your pattern is to wait for a bus that never turns up and then you go round to the bus station and say, 'Wait a minute, where's this bus,' and they say, 'Hello, it's the Eiffel Tower – off. I don't want passengers like you who are gonna wait around for five years.' As opposed to you say, 'Look, my needs are important to me' – are they, by the way?

Ruth: Absolutely.

Windy: Right, but you say that but you've got to act it. You've got to implement that. That's maybe another bit of learning, that, 'My needs are important to me and, if I'm not getting it, I'm going to raise it as carefully as I can but I'm gonna raise it and see what happens and then take it forward on that basis. And, if after a while I'm not getting what I want when I've had a reasonable amount of chance of getting it, it's probably not for me and then I move on.'

Ruth: Yeah.

Windy: Now, is that a good way forward for you?

Ruth: I feel it's quite hard.

Windy: In what sense hard?

Ruth: As in, if somebody does something that I don't like and I have a discussion around that and they become attacking or dismissive or that's their way of managing, that I would just go. I find that quite hard.

Windy: You might then raise that and say, 'Look, I don't want you to shout at me. Can we find a different way?' and, if they can't find a different way, then you can go. You don't go at the first sign of things. You try to work it out, but I'm just saying that you've removed yourself from a relationship in your waiting; you're not there. You're not on the sidelines waiting for change to occur. And it doesn't and you say, 'Well, maybe he hasn't settled yet. Maybe I've got to give him some more space,' and things like that, as opposed to getting in there and deal with the conflict. I mean, we're not talking about physical conflict, are we?

[It would have been better if I had asked something like, 'When it becomes clear that you are not going to get your desire for closeness met, how can you leave the relationship so that you aren't being hard?']

Ruth: No. I mean, I left. In the beginning, I actually went back to my house quite a few times 'cos I said, 'I can't speak to you. You're upsetting me and I'm gonna go back to the house.' So, in the beginning, probably in the first six months I left probably once a month.

Windy: Well, that's telling you something, isn't it?

Ruth: Yes, and the outcome of that was I got bought an Oscar with 'The World's Biggest Drama Queen' on it and I found it really insulting, and they thought that was really funny.

Windy: And you stayed?

Ruth: And I stayed.

Windy: So, what is it about you that puts up with so much crap?

Ruth: … [*Pause*] I think my training's done a lot of it, Windy, to be honest.

Windy: They train you as a counsellor and say, 'No. 1: Take crap in relationships. Now you're a counsellor, you've got to take the crap.' Really?

Ruth: I think I've gone the other way: I'm too compassionate.

Windy: No, you're not compassionate enough.

Ruth: Right.

Windy: To yourself.

[*Ruth believes that being compassionate involves giving people opportunities to change due to the struggles they have faced, and awaiting their transformation. By doing this, I highlight that she is not being compassionate towards herself and what matters to her. You will notice that I employ the terms 'editing yourself out' and 'editing yourself in' to illustrate what she has done (edited herself out) and what she could do (editing herself in).*]

Ruth: And you are correct. I met with a new supervisor on Tuesday and they said to me, 'You don't value yourself at all. What's going on?' and that was through a questionnaire, and I was like, 'What?'

Windy: Whereabouts do you live, by the way?

Ruth: I'm in Somerset.

Windy: How do you meet people?

Ruth: I socialise. I go out and about. Aside from my practice, I do community work at the hospital. I've got lots of friends. I'm always socialising. I sea swim. I go to the gym.

Windy: Right, so the chances are with all these activities you might meet somebody who has prospects for a romantic relationship, right? Now, what are you gonna do differently this time?

Ruth: … I think I'm gonna be very suspicious when it happens. What am I going to do differently? Maybe find out about them.

Windy: Right, find out about them is always a good idea. Yeah, what else?

Ruth: I've done this before with the other chap; he just changed when I moved in. Maybe not move in.

Windy: Well, fine. Or move in and, once he changes, try to deal with it but then move out.

Ruth: I think moving forward… [*pause*] just giving someone a chance, 'cos this chap has been in and out of my life, as I say, since the 80s; there's a lot of history there from schooldays, but I didn't really know him. So, I guess the key here is to know somebody, because you can go on dates. I can talk for Britain, Windy, I could fill the whole date by myself.

Windy: Yeah, but that's not the point. You want to find out about them.

Ruth: Yeah, find out about them, their likes and dislikes.

Windy: Right, and what about the bit about your needs?

Ruth: I don't know if I'd bring that up on a date.

Windy: No, not on a date, but in terms of what's important to you. Are you gonna edit that out or are you gonna edit that back in?

Ruth: I will edit it back in because it's very important. I'm not getting any younger, and I don't want to end my days on my own. I've got a lot to give.

Windy: And what's gonna happen when you're not getting your needs met? What are you going to do then?

Ruth: … [*Pause*] I guess I'm gonna have to bring it up as soon as.

Windy: Why do you have to guess?

Ruth: Because I know I'm really bad at it.

Windy: How can you get good at it?

Ruth: Write them a letter and run.

[*I don't think I have adequately addressed her fear of conflict in this session.*]

Windy: Well, yeah, you could do that or you could recognise that you become good at something by recognising it's difficult but keep doing it and learning along the way.

Ruth: Yeah. I guess practice makes perfect, doesn't it?

Windy: Right, and, if they're highly aggressive towards you, then that gives you feedback; that's getting to know them.

Ruth: Yes. I wouldn't say people were aggressive towards me. I would say they were more disengaged.

Windy: Right. And, if they're disengaged as a response, what then?

Ruth: Then it's just not worth pursuing.

Windy: Right, OK. So, there you've got a way forward for yourself.

Ruth: Yeah. I am writing notes. And I guess as well, Windy, I actually don't take dating seriously. I've never been on a dating app or anything like that. And I've been asked out for drinks quite a lot through my work and I just brush it off. I don't give people a chance because I was always hooked on my ex-partner, I think.

Windy: Right. Well, now you're unhooked.

Ruth: I'm unhooked.

Windy: And maybe also you may want to revisit the amount of time you're giving people to settle.

Ruth: Yeah, because I think I'm quite easy to live with. Someone that's quite black and white may think that I'm not easy to live with because I like to read, I like to study. Maybe I'm emotionally unavailable as well. But I will drop what I'm doing for the other person. I seem to attract very masculine males, very alpha males.

Windy: Is that a good thing or a bad thing for you?

Ruth: I think now it's a bad thing, Windy, because we never gel.

Windy: So, there's the learning. Are you attracted to alpha males?

Ruth: Well, they're quite persistent. I think that's the attractiveness of being wooed, because you don't get wooed very much nowadays. It's a stalking law now, isn't it?

Windy: Well, don't forget the old adage: if you're wooed you may end up being screwed.

Ruth: Ooh, I didn't know that one.

Windy: Well, I've just made it up. That's why. If you're wooed by the wrong person, you're gonna end up being screwed, 'cos you seem to edit yourself out. 'If somebody's really persistent, then I'll have a relationship with them. Not what I want. What I want, I don't want an alpha male anymore whether they're persistent or not. It doesn't work for me anymore.'

Ruth: No, it doesn't.

Windy: That's you bringing you back into it, where you've edited yourself out.

Ruth: Yeah. My sister said that, if you want to catch a good fish, you have to change the bait. I don't want to see myself as bait, though, but maybe.

Windy: But you've got to throw the rod into the water first, 'cos the bait may not be on the rod. But also the question is, you could throw the fish back. And, if you throw the fish back and the same fish comes back time and time again, that's not a good reason to have a relationship with the fish.

Ruth: It isn't, and I think – I know that my life is enmeshed with my practice. I know it is because it is pity, it is compassion. I do give people a lot of chances because I know everybody's got their own struggles. And maybe that's what it is. Maybe my professional and personal boundaries are really enmeshed at the moment.

Windy: I think you may need to say, 'Yeah, I do want to give people a chance, but I'm editing myself back in there. What chance am I gonna give them given the fact that I have needs that I want to get fulfilled?' not, 'How much time do I give them because I'm compassionate towards them and I feel sorry for them and, oh, where's me? Oh, that doesn't matter because I'm busy doing the compassion and the pity.' If you edit yourself back in, then you'll be able to answer the question about how much time is healthy for you to give them. Not for them but for you.

Ruth: Yeah. You're exactly right there. Things have to change 'cos I don't have many, as you say, five- and ten-year increments left to meet a partner. I'm not desperate to meet anyone, Windy, at all. It's not that I'm sat here and, 'Oh, I need to be with someone.'

Windy: No, that's fine, but you do want to meet somebody and, if you learn from some of the things that we've spoken about today going forward, it will be interesting to see what happens.

Ruth: Yeah. Yes, it would, because my children are grown now, and I think that's a lot of it as well, just being in a family environment, which is quite weird because this person's family didn't talk to them. So, we never had. It was still my family environment. So, they were just there.

Windy: So, let's have a look at what we've talked about. What's your summary of what we spoke about and what are you gonna take away?

[I am sensing that we are approaching the end of the conversation, so I ask Ruth for her summary and her takeaways.]

Ruth: My summary that I have, that we've spoken about is to not wait five years for a bus. If conflict happens or if things aren't going quite well and I want a discussion around, 'My needs aren't being met here. I'm feeling quite lonely or quite dismissed,' if that's met with resistance or defensiveness, then that's quite a red flag, and not to let that go on, basically.

Windy: Yeah, quite, absolutely. And what else?

Ruth: I think to put me first.

Windy: Yep.

Ruth: To know myself. Maybe I need to go on a wild woman camp or something to really know my desires and my wants for life, and put it out there that, if I do meet somebody in the future, make sure it's the right fit, because life is quite precious. I don't want to waste any more. I do feel like I have wasted, and I don't want to live in regret, but I do feel like I've wasted many, many years in this relationship with somebody who has no respect or regard for me.

Windy: What did he get out of it?

Ruth: I think he got out the fact that, so in his house he used to have his pals living and I turned it into a home and the spare room was my dressing room and we had dinner on a Sunday. So, he had a family environment, but I don't think he actually wanted that, to be honest. I think he had a sense of security. I think he was honouring his mum's memory, 'cos his mum really liked me; I got on really well with her when I was a teenager. And I think to the outside world he was settled. But to the inside of us, there was no relationship.

Windy: Is he likely to make any attempts to resurrect the relationship?

Ruth: I don't think so. Not now. I've not spoken to him for three weeks. He's not contacted me.

Windy: But, if he does, would you be interested in doing that?

Ruth: Never. Not now.

Windy: That's definitive.

Ruth: Not since Paris, Windy.

Windy: Yes. We'll always have Paris. Where does that come from? *Casablanca.*

Ruth: I just remember the couples' reactions. They heard what he said and they were like aghast. And I remember standing there thinking, 'Wow. If this wasn't funny, it would be humiliating.' But I'm not ego-led, but I think it just flawed me, to be honest.

Windy: Well, you certainly got an 'eye-ful' of his bluntness. By the way, I think you should get yourself one of these.

Ruth: A red flag.

               [*I have several visual props that I use in my online work. A red flag is one of these props.*]

Windy: That's the one.

Ruth: Have it in my handbag.

Windy: That's right. As a reminder.

Ruth: I may just do that.

Windy: Yeah. I'm a great believer in these little reminders. Now, do you see any obstacles for you to implement this?

Ruth: … Ooh, do I see obstacles? I think in pictures and I'm just trying to think about going on a date with somebody and being that person that I don't want to be: that assertive female that says, 'This is me, this is my needs, blah blah blah.'

Windy: So, what is it about being an assertive female that you shrink away from?

Ruth: What do I shrink away from? Again, I think it's a form of conflict. I have two sisters, they're very businesslike. They're in their 70s now and retired but they're still very matriarchal, and I'm not. And, when they say, even in a shop, 'No, I'll give you half the money for that. I'm not paying full price,' and I literally want to hide and I'll leave.

Windy: There's a restaurant that we go to in Madeira sometimes and they have dish called Octopus Our Way. So maybe you could think about Assertiveness Your Way. You seem to have reacted to that assertiveness by not being assertive rather than saying, 'Well,

I can still be assertive but I can do it in a gentler, less harsh way.'

Ruth: Yes, and I think when I've tried to be assertive especially in this relationship and ones before, I'm not heard.

[On her pre-session form, Ruth indicated that her strengths include being assertive, strong, and compassionate. I wish I had referred to this here. I could have said something like, 'On your pre-session form, you said that being assertive and being strong were two of your strengths. How could you bring these strengths to discussions like these?']

Windy: But that's good evidence for you, isn't it?

Ruth: Yes.

Windy: What does that tell you?

Ruth: It says I'm not assertive at all.

Windy: No. What it says to me is that you don't matter.

Ruth: Yeah.

Windy: Do you want to matter to somebody?

Ruth: Absolutely.

Windy: Right. So that's a sign that you may not matter if the person's not gonna listen to you and not hear you. And, so, if you don't assert yourself, you'll never find that out.

Ruth: No, you're right.

Windy: Any other obstacles?

Ruth: Any other obstacles? ... [*Pause*] Effect on family, I think, because whatever they say to me I don't hear them either.

Windy: What do you mean effect on family?

Ruth: So, throughout this relationship my family, especially my children, were like, 'Why? This person's just not a nice person. What are you doing? My lovely mum, what are you doing?' and I'm like, 'He's really nice.' So, I guess it's the rose-tinted glasses thing with me as well. Maybe my family should meet the person long before I date them because they know me, don't they? I sort of had five parents growing up.

Windy: They may be nice but are they meeting your needs? Just because they're nice doesn't mean you have to have a relationship with them, 'cos they're nice. The question is it's niceness plus needs being met rather than niceness on its own, it sounds to me.

Ruth: I mean, for me I'm just happy when I'm out doing things. So, yeah, I don't put enough importance, maybe, on going out for a date. To me it's just I'm out and I go out anyway.

Windy: The point is, it sounds like you do want to have a relationship with somebody, but, as you say, you're not desperate, which is good. You are able to go out anyway, and I think that's fine. But now it's a bit like this session has taught you how to drive. You know what you need now?

Ruth: A car.

Windy: And to drive it. So, we need some men to practise on.

Ruth: OK. So, I am going out tonight to see a play about grief, and there's a fake wake afterwards with the actors.

Windy: A fake wake?

Ruth: A fake wake.

Windy: Not a fake shake.

Ruth: No. A fake funeral, fake wake. It's a play. It's part of *Good Grief Weston-Super-Mare* and there is a soiree afterwards. So maybe I'll get chatting. Maybe not talk to someone at the bar and tell them all my needs.

Windy: No, exactly. OK, that sounds good. So, I'll contact you in three months and see how you get on.

Ruth: Thank you, Windy. I think I will put my dating head on, even to just go out, I'm not even going to say for friendship because this is where I go wrong. I'm not their friend. I'm their partner. So maybe I'll go to some speed dating outside of Weston, by the way, not where I am. Maybe I'll do some speed dating and meeting someone and practise my worth.

Windy: That's right. Exactly.

Ruth's Follow-up Questionnaire

Date: 04-01-25

Question	Response
1. What progress did you make on the issue that you brought to the session. Indicate the amount of progress you have made on this issue by using a 0% (no progress) – 100% (problem solved) scale.	**Issue Brought to the Session (Please name this):** Unrequited Love **Amount of progress made:** 70% **Factors that helped me make progress:** Acknowledging that my time is precious and my personal boundaries are important. Assisting me to understand that my repeated patterns of behaviour within relationships were caused by me not wanting to enter into conflict with my partners, which led to my own suffering. **Factors that were absent that could have helped me make more progress:** Noting the importance of being future-focused around personal goals and achievements

2. Did you make any progress on other issues that you have that you did not bring to our session? Please elaborate.	I have factored in more time for self-care and doing things that bring me joy.
3. How would you describe your relationship with Windy Dryden in the session?	I found Windy to be warm, knowledgeable and challenging without being directly critical. I would describe our relationship as being fluid and yet boundaried at the same time.
4. What, if anything, did Windy Dryden do during the session that was helpful to you?	Windy gave another perspective on my issues that were not yet in my awareness. My friends now carry a red flag in their handbags to alert me to unsuitable dating choices.
5. What, if anything, did Windy Dryden do during the session that was unhelpful to you?	I cannot think of anything as I felt the session went well, and I processed it a lot over the weeks following.

6. How helpful did you find the pre-session form if you were sent one? Please elaborate.	I found this helpful as it gave me time to think in depth about my issue before the session. I also believe it gave Windy an insight into the problem so it was helpful to establish a sense of mutual understanding within the therapeutic relationship
7. How helpful did you find the audio-recording of your session? Please elaborate.	I found the audio-recording extremely helpful, as I listened to the content of the session in the days following, and was able to process my feelings and take action.
8. How helpful did you find the transcript of your sessions? Please elaborate.	I found it a little helpful, although it did not take into account the humour within the session.

9. How does Single-Session Therapy compare with other therapies that you have had? Please elaborate.	Single-Session Therapy is an effective problem-solving tool. It does not look deeply into the root causes of issues, but helps to find strategies for coping within current situations that are drawn from past experiences.
10. What improvements, if any, do you think need to be made to the Single-Session Therapy framework?	I think it is a good, solid framework for today's fast paced lifestyles.
11. Please give any additional feedback that your responses to the questions above have not covered.	I would just like to take this opportunity to thank Windy for assisting me with my new sense of empowerment around the issue of feeling unrequited love within relationships, as I now have a deeper understanding of the importance of my own needs and desires, and will be proactive in meeting these needs within future relationships.

My Reflections and Summary

On her pre-session form, Ruth stated that she wanted to understand why she stays in loveless relationships and why it takes her many years to walk away from them. Ruth seemed to have obtained what she hoped for from the session regarding this understanding. She said she has learned that her time and personal boundaries are important and that she had let her fear of conflict lead her to remain in stagnant relationships. Interestingly, I felt that I did not adequately address Ruth's fear of conflict in the session, but perhaps from Ruth's perspective, I did or that she was able to work this through after the session. On the 0–100% progress scale, Ruth thought she had made 70% progress towards problem resolution and in other areas of her life, she said that she had 'factored in more time for self-care and doing things that bring me joy'.

I think I did a reasonably good job in the session and, unlike with Sarah Louise (see Chapter 2), I did not cover too much ground. I think the salient issues for Ruth emerged from our conversation in a relaxed way, and I did not have to introduce any concepts from my preferred therapeutic orientation (REBT) into the session. I felt that I did not adequately deal with Ruth's fear of conflict, but it seems that this was not a concern for her.

In terms of our therapeutic relationship, Ruth said that she found me to be 'warm, knowledgeable and challenging without being directly critical.' She described our relationship as fluid yet boundaried at the same time. She also appreciated my use of humour, which she found evident in the recording but not in the transcript.

Regarding the pre-session form, recording, and transcript, Ruth stated the following. She mentioned that she found the pre-session form useful, as it allowed her time to think deeply about her issue before the session and informed me of what she wanted to discuss. She found the recording of our session useful, but the transcript was less so.

The only factor she believed was missing that could have been beneficial was being more 'future-focused around personal goals and achievements'.

4

Dealing with Betrayal

Date: 10-10-24
Time: 43 mins 31 secs

Cat's Pre-Session Form

On her pre-session form, Cat stated that she wanted to focus on the impact of experiences of betrayal in romantic relationships on her ability to be genuinely optimistic about the likelihood of finding a loving long-term relationship.

Cat said that recently, she realised with great sadness, that she does not believe she will have another good love relationship in her life even though it is what she longs for. Her *goal* was to have made some inroads in breaking down that barrier by the end of the session and being able to embody a sense of possibility instead.

In response to the question, 'How have you tied to deal with the issue up to this point?', Cat said, 'Personal therapy, reading relevant thinking about the issue, moving to live in a retreat centre in California to escape the British culture that seemed to be giving me the same man repeatedly, becoming much happier in myself and less needy of a relationship, training as a psychotherapist and recently as a couple therapist

From the list of forms of *help* she was hoping I could provide her, Cat chose 'Help me to solve an emotional or behavioural problem; help me get unstuck'.

Cat listed her inner resources as knowing herself well, being able to be honest with and about herself, believing herself to be lovable and likeable, being able to tolerate confrontation and express healthy anger and as a result of a psychotic breakdown earlier in her life realising that she is resilient and courageous.

The Session

Windy: OK then, Cat, so what's your understanding of the purpose of our conversation today?

Cat: Well, it's around the topic of betrayal, but that's a wide one in some ways. And I think what I said I wanted to focus on in the session was my experience of betrayal in the context of romantic relationships and its impact on, I feel, my ability to feel genuinely optimistic about getting into a healthy, long-term relationship at this point in my life, which is what I would like.

Windy: Have you had one before?

Cat: Yes. I had one for seven years, which wasn't really a very good relationship, but that's the relationship in which I had my daughter, which is why it lasted for as long as it did. And I had a very good one, which was about five or six years, and that ended because we reached the deal-breaking situation of he didn't want to have children, and I did.

Windy: Right, OK. So, you have had the experience of actually having a relationship with men that were suitable for you?

Cat: Yeah.

Windy: And I guess you've had relationships with men that haven't been suitable for you.

Cat: Yes, and it took me a long time to realise that I… think a lot of the problem has been that I don't think I'm attracted to people that are ever gonna give me what I want.

Windy: OK.

Cat: So, I think my attachment style is preoccupied, and I tend to go for avoidant men who mirror my father's attachment style.

Windy: OK. The operative word there is 'tend to'.

Cat: 'Tend to', yes.

Windy: That means that you still have a choice.

Cat: Yes … although I would say it doesn't end up feeling like that, but I totally agree with you. Yes.

Windy: The question is whether it feels like that depends upon whether you act on that or not.

Cat: Yes.... [*Pause*] Yes, and I have got a lot better at identifying the signs earlier on.... In fact, the last long-term relationship I was in, he wasn't avoidant; he was actually disorganised, which is worse in many ways, but anyway. But ... I have just noticed that ... [*pause*] what I tend to be attracted to is, it generally turns out to be, an avoidant attachment style.

Windy: And, on the basis of hindsight, do you think you could have spotted that earlier?

Cat: Do I think I could've spotted it earlier? ... [*Long pause*] Yes. In fact, the last relationship I was in, I took a very conscious decision to get into a relationship where I realised very quickly the person was avoidant, but I decided that ... I would just enjoy what was on offer in that relationship, because at the time, I had just gone back to completing my training as a psychotherapist and had very little time and was also a single parent. And so, I wasn't really looking for the kind of relationship I'm now looking for anyway. So, I took a very conscious decision around that.

Windy: Yeah. So, you noticed that he was emotionally unavailable, you decided to pursue it because it suited your life where you were.

Cat: Absolutely.

Windy: But, thinking about relationships that you might develop in the future, that's not what you want even though you might start off becoming drawn to an emotionally unavailable male as it may turn out that way. Is that what you're saying?

[*Up to now, Cat has been giving me the context of her issue, focusing on her past experiences. At this point, I ask about the future.*]

Cat: Yes. I really would like... the experience of ... being in a relationship with somebody who isn't unavailable. And this only occurs in my romantic relationships. I have very good close friendships. I am perfectly capable relationally in every other area of my life.

Windy: Right, OK. So, would you be able to, based on what you've identified in a potential male partner, spot the signs and recognise, 'Yeah, I may be drawn to this, but it's not good for me'?

Cat: Yes.

Windy: 'And, therefore, I'm not gonna continue with that.'

Cat: Yes.

Windy: Right, OK. So that's the important step, isn't it, the realisation?

[*I want to underscore Cat's ability to recognise her tendency to be drawn to unavailable men and choose, now, not to pursue a relationship with such a man.*]

Cat: Yes. Well, yes, but this implies that I'm in a position where I could meet any number of men of all kinds of attachment persuasions, which ... [*pause*] I suppose, in theory, given all the ways we have of doing that these days, is correct. But the reality is not that correct.

Windy: The point is, statistically, the bigger the sample, unless you go to www.emotionally avoidantmen.com, the chances of you actually finding somebody increase with an increased sample size.

Cat: Yes.

Windy: So, are you willing to do that?

Cat: I'm willing to do that. I think my key issue ... and it's one of the things I find very frustrating about myself, I think on one level I'm a very self-aware person and I've done a hell of a lot of therapy, but I think it's taken me a long time to realise just how responsible

I am in this ... just how big a part I play in this.

Windy: And what part do you play, have you discovered?

Cat: Well, I make choices that aren't helpful for me and then I stick with those choices. I really don't think I would do this anymore, and I have evidence that I haven't done it in recent years, but I have tended to stick with somebody who's avoidant with that magical thinking of I can be the one to change them, I can be the one to rescue them, I can be the one to...

Windy: Cure cancer? Cure baldness?

Cat: Yes.

Windy: And all those types of stuff. OK, but you say you're no longer like that. So, what's different? How are you different?

Cat: I think I'm more self-aware. More tired. I've got a much bigger 'I can't be arsed' driver than I used to have around all that stuff, which actually is quite helpful, I think, because I think I ... have had a personality makeup which was to like to push on closed doors, for some reason. And that I have changed. I think I've seen that as a sort of challenge. I'm not interested in that any more.

Windy: So, you could bring the old Cat to this issue or the new Cat.

Cat: I'm not interested in bringing the old Cat to this issue, actually, any more. I'm really not.

Windy: Good. One of the things you're asking for here is being able to embody a sense of possibility in being able to find somebody who will give you what you're looking for. What would give you a sign that you were taking that away by the end of the session?

[I contrast the old Cat with the new Cat, and she says she wants to bring the new Cat to deal with this issue. I then refer back to her pre-session form and read out her goal, to remind us both of the goal-directed nature of the conversation.]

Cat: I don't know. I know it sounds strange to say this, but in filling in your form was almost the moment where I thought, I mean, intellectually, yeah, sure, but emotionally I really don't believe this is gonna happen for me, and that's a big problem.

Windy: Well, do you regard yourself as being open-minded?

Cat: Yes.

Windy: So, are you willing to bring your open mind to that statement?

         [*I immediately respond to Cat's pessimism by inviting her to be open-minded about the possibility of meeting someone.*]

Cat: Yes.

Windy: That wasn't the purpose of the form.

Cat: No, I realise that, but I think in these processes of reflecting on these things, sometimes ... yeah.

Windy: So, what would give you a sense that, OK, on reflection, it may happen for you, if you bring the new Cat to the table with a big enough sample?

Cat: ... I think ... [*pause*] feeling a sense of... maybe a beginning of a connection with an individual, or several individuals, that feel like that could be something worth pursuing there.

Windy: How are you gonna bring that about?

Cat: So, I have done, over time ... I don't know whether I'd call it 'a lot of', I've had periods of doing online dating ... even before it was online, in fact. It was partly the process of starting it again about a month ago that made me realise how negative I actually feel about it, because I think I'd thought, 'Oh well, if I decide to do this again, I can do it in a quite positive way.' And I didn't find that that was what happened.

Windy: What happened?

Cat: What happened was I ... [*pause*] really thought about, 'I need to approach this differently.' I thought I would try and do it differently, not pay much attention to what somebody looked like other than extremes of any kind, and instead focus on the kinds of things people said. So, for example, I put in certain filters like: I'm only going to filter people that are interested in a long-term relationship; I'm only going to focus on – or at least say that because that's all you can filter, what people actually put or don't put – it was more I'm going to be quite ... formulaic around how I go about this, whilst trying not to be rigid.

Windy: Right. And what happened?

Cat: So far ... it's been disappointing.... I'm not quite sure why, as in one of the sites I chose to go on is a site I've never used before and I have talked to a couple of friends who've used it and I think there might be something about that particular site, but what I found with that was that virtually nobody has shown any interest in me. So that's ... inevitably not very encouraging.

Windy: No.

Cat: I'm sure you know enough about these things to know that there are certain things that happen which are frustrating, like you think why would anyone put a photograph of themselves that's 10 years old? Why would anyone set themselves up in that way? But a lot of people do.

Windy: Do you mean 10 years younger than they are?

Cat: Yeah. I don't want, if I get on a video call with somebody, to watch their face drop. At least they're getting what they were expecting, whether that's bad or not. So it surprises me the number of people that seem to be willing to do that.

Windy: The point is, I guess it's a numbers game – you may be lucky and meet somebody on your first throw.

Cat: Exactly, and that's exactly what it is: it's a numbers game.

Windy: And it may well be that the site that you're talking about is not for you, and other sites may be. You need to, I guess, experiment with that. But it sounds like you're prepared to go forward. And I think, in a way, going forward with the idea that, 'I may not find anybody, but I may.'

Cat: Yeah.

Windy: I guess that's the only thing that you can do, isn't it?

Cat: It is, and I keep thinking you only need one.

Windy: Exactly.

Cat: And it is a numbers game, you're right, and … the statistical reality is that where I live, doing the job I do at my age, it is really the only way. It's not the only way to meet somebody, of course, but, if you actually want to up the chance of it happening, it really is the only way, I really do think.

Windy: Yeah. There may be opportunities elsewhere. I don't know what you like to do, but often, if you like art, for example, you go to galleries. The opportunity may be to meet people there. So, there's virtual life and there's actual life.

Cat: There is.

Windy: They both may give you opportunities.

Cat: Yeah, but I think the online approach is at least it's a more directive possibility.

Windy: Yeah. You see, what you're in control of is how you portray yourself, isn't it?

Cat: Yeah.

Windy: You're not in control of how other people choose to portray themselves.

Cat: No.

Windy: But I guess, when somebody comes on looking 10 years older than they are, your choice is to pursue or not pursue that.

Cat: Yes.

Windy: But I guess the things that you are in control of are which site you go on, how often you go on it, what you choose to put on it, the transition between typing and meeting, whether there's gonna be a video or whatever it is. All those things you're in control of.

    [*It would have been better if I had asked Cat what she was in control regarding online dating.*]

Cat: Yes. And I'm pretty, I think … clear about what each of these communications, what it gives you, and so I'm quite clear that photographs of people you don't know tell you remarkably little about them, which isn't something you ever have to know unless you're looking at photographs of strangers in a weird way. But they don't tell you much. They don't tell you that much, photos. And what somebody writes on a profile also doesn't tell you very much. And, so the way I go about it is quite quickly suggesting a conversation because that to me is where you start getting some reality, in my experience.

I've learnt a bit over the years about myself and – it doesn't really matter what other people are doing – about what works and doesn't work for me. What I don't like is, I don't want – although I think I also probably don't do this so much anymore, but there's an awful lot of room for building up fantasy when you are in the space where you don't know much about somebody. So, I'm not interested in exchanging loads and loads and loads of texts. Sometimes, there are people who actually don't have any intention of ever meeting anybody.

Windy: Exactly, yeah. They're playing with it.

Cat: I cut to the chase very quickly, and some people probably don't like that.

Windy: Well, then, that's fine.

Cat: But then I think, 'Well, you're not for me. Good luck.'

Windy: Exactly. So, it sounds like, if you maximise the variables that are in your control, which are: how you navigate yourself on online sites like this, that you're pursuing a certain way of working which is, 'Let's cut to the chase, let's see what happens,' that's fine. The bit which says, 'OK, I'm gonna bring the new Cat to this. I'm gonna be aware of signs, when I do meet people, of emotional unavailability and I have a choice at that point: I could either choose to bring the old Cat back or keep the new Cat to the fore.' That's your choice.

   If you were to put that together and say that's what you're going to do as an action plan, does that increase the sense of possibility for you, or are there some other ingredients that need to be added to this particular dish?

Cat: Well, it does intellectually, but I think some of my stuckness is something around what I've come to believe about myself. I think from the fact that I'm nearly 60, and I'm not in a long-term relationship, and I am a single parent ...

Windy: And what have you come to believe about yourself, about those factors?

Cat: I think for a long time I believed that it was as if there was some magic code that everyone else had been given and I hadn't.... [*Pause*] That doesn't feel very real to me anymore, but there is something about... [pause], it's not quite as simple as I don't seem to be as desirable as other people, but, when I say it, that actually feels now outdated too. So, I don't know whether it's part of me that hasn't caught up with an older bit, if that makes sense. I don't really know what keeps me....

Windy: It may well be that your stuckness is that you're operating as if these factors are current, and they're not. And, therefore, if you act as if they're not current – let's even assume the worst temporarily – even if it's true that you're less desirable than other people would be, so what? The same is true: you only need to meet one person who's interested in you.

Cat: That is very true, yes.

Windy: So, you can regard these obstacles as things to not jump over or you could jump over them and, in the jumping over them, you increase the chances of the possibility happening for you. If you don't jump over the hurdles, you'll increase the chances of, 'There's not much of a possibility for me.'

Cat: Yeah.

Windy: So, even the possibilities are in your control.

Cat: Say more about that.

Windy: Well, through your behaviour. If you avoid going over obstacles, it becomes harder in your mind. You jump over them, you increase the chances of it. The other thing that you're not bringing to the table, because in that short summary about yourself, it was more demographic factors of age and things like that, but what do you have to offer somebody?

Cat: That didn't seem very relevant to your pre-session form, in my defence, but what do I have to offer someone? Actually, quite a lot, I would say.

Windy: Right. And do you think about that going forward?

Cat: Do I think about it?

Windy: Yeah. When you're thinking about possibilities, are you saying, 'OK, I could look at it in terms of let's have a look at what might count against me or I could recognise, yes, those are facts as well, but let's also have a look at what's in my favour'?

Cat: Yeah.

Windy: Do you do much of that?

Cat: Do I do much reflecting on that? ... [*Pause*] Probably not that much. I tend to be much more aware of the gap. I'm not a glass-half-empty person particularly, in general. It's weird, I really am very different in this particular area of my life.

Windy: Sure, but all that means is that you're not using things that you use in other areas of your life, you haven't used it as much in this area of your life.

Cat: I'm socially quite a confident person. I'm pretty clear. I can pretty much talk to anyone. So, I'm not shy. I'm not awkward or any of those things. And, also, I only ever get involved in doing this online stuff when I'm feeling resilient, because I am very aware that it is not helpful to do it when you're not feeling resilient. And that's what I always advise other people as well.

Windy: Right. You're taking care of yourself as well. I was going to say, there's a famous cartoon in the single-session therapy community where this doctor looks at an x-ray and says to the patient, 'The good news is there's nothing wrong with you that what's right with you can't cure.' So, there's nothing that you can't bring to the table here that can't help to deal with the obstacle and the stuckness if you choose to recognise that you can bring the half-full part of yourself into this area; you can transfer it into this area.

[*This is an important strategy in SST. I am encouraging Cat to bring her strengths in other areas of her life to online dating.*]

Cat: Yes.

Windy: It doesn't come naturally to you, but you can still bring it to the area and do it until it becomes naturally at those times when you're feeling resilient.

Cat: Yeah. I think that's a sort of self-protection/defence thing.

Windy: What is?

Cat: That… not bringing that glass-half-full part of myself, I think that's what brings about that attitude.

Windy: How does not bringing it help you?

Cat: I don't think it does. I think it's … an unhelpful behaviour. But that's really useful

to think about that. I talk about this when I'm
doing therapy with people all the time, about:
well, that weird thing if I don't dare to hope
for something isn't gonna make any
difference to the outcome. It's that you think
that but it's that weird magical negative
thinking we all do. And I think that's what
I'm saying, I think that's what I do with this,
probably.

Windy: Yeah. And now that you've recognised that,
you have a choice to continue to do it or not
to continue to do it.

Cat: No, it's really unhelpful.

Windy: But it still might be something which crops
up first. Another principle of single-session
therapy is don't be overly concerned about
what comes up first. Help the person to
respond to what comes up first so that they
take away what comes up second.

[*Another path I could have taken here was to
invite Cat to look at what she called the 'self-
protection/defence' thing related to her
bringing a glass-half-empty stance to online
dating.*]

Cat: OK.

Windy: OK?

Cat: Yes.

Windy: So, if we were to add that to the mix, which is that you're gonna bring, not only the new Cat in terms of spotting the emotionally avoidant men, you're gonna play the numbers game, you're gonna emphasise the things that are in your control, you're gonna bring the half-full Cat to this even though the half-empty Cat might crop up first. What else might actually help you to leave our discussion with a sense of increased possibility?

Cat: … [*Long pause*] I think something you said earlier about, 'Well, that might not be the site for you.' … I think … [*pause*] trying something for a bit and giving myself permission to give up on that and try and different tack rather than thinking I'm just not trying hard enough or I'm not whatever. That feels a bit more freeing, actually.

Windy: Right, OK. Yeah, allowing yourself to be clear about just how much you are going to follow things through.

Cat: I've just realised something as we've been talking which is I feel … this task of finding a mate is really hard work … and … that's not said from a logical, intellectual place. It feels emotionally like very hard work, even though actually I haven't even engaged with it that much yet.

Windy: Right, OK. And what stance are you gonna take on that statement that it's hard work?

Cat: Well, I think ... [*pause*], I'm not sure that's actually borne out in reality. I think it's more the heaviness with which I approach it's the problem, in a sense. And, actually, it isn't particularly hard work. I mean, I'm not a doom-scroller by nature, but it's certainly no worse than any of that.

Windy: No, but, again, if you allow yourself to have that as a first response, but it's not your last response.

Cat: Yes. It's so useful.... [*Pause*] I haven't really talked about my process around this, truthfully, this time around with anyone, so I'm talking to you about it now.... Because I think it's something that can easily bring up quite a lot of shame for me and all sorts of other things.

Windy: Shame in what sense?

Cat: I've got myself to a place of feeling like a generally quite competent human being in enough areas of my life, and this is an area of my life that I don't feel like a competent human being in.

Windy: Yet.

Cat: Yet.

Windy: What's shameful about that?

Cat: ... [*Long pause*] Intellectually, my brain goes quiet when you ask that question.

Windy: What about emotionally then?

Cat: But there's all sorts of uncomfortable feelings that come up when you say that.

Windy: Like what?

Cat: ... [*Pause*] I think it makes me feel sad. Sad.

Windy: Sad is different from shame, though, isn't it?

Cat: It is different from shame. I feel sad.

Windy: Shame is more about your view of you because you've fallen short of this competent ideal that you have in the rest of your life. Whereas, if you can allow yourself to be a person who can be competent and not so competent, and that you can address the not-so-competent in ways that you could grow in competence. But it is sad in the sense that you haven't got what you want yet.

Cat: Yes.

Windy: And you may never get it. That would be sad, but you may get it.

Cat: Yes.

Windy: Come back in 20 years' time and we will find out which one that was.

Cat: I would really like, in 20 years' time, if I'm still alive, which I hope I will be, actually – I'll only be 80 then – that I would be with someone and that I would be able to say, 'You know what–'

Windy: There's nothing which you have said today which means that you couldn't achieve that.

Cat: OK.... [*Pause*] Yeah.

Windy: If you're willing to be aware how your mind works in this area and be able to have a good response to areas of your mind which are stopping you from moving forward and getting what you want.

Cat: The thing that came up for me just then was all I need to do is to get out of my own way.

Windy: Yes, but being understanding of how you get in your own way and then to recognise that you can understand that but you could then respond in ways that have a different pathway for you forward.

[I am extensively employing the first reaction – second response strategy with Cat, as she seems to resonate with this concept. This strategy conveys that if we acknowledge and comprehend our initial, typically unhealthy reaction, we can respond to it in a healthy manner.]

Cat: Yes.

Windy: One thing we haven't spoken about – maybe we don't need to speak about it now, I don't, it's up to you – is betrayal and how betrayal might be an obstacle to this.

[Cat chose 'betrayal' from a list of adversities that she wanted to discuss with me, but aside from a brief mention of this issue at the beginning of our session, it did not make an appearance. That's fine by me, but I wanted to provide Cat with the opportunity to discuss it if she wished to.]

Cat: Yes, and that's an interesting one in that I think its relevance is just that it adds to the … *[long pause]* want to go there/don't want to go there, push/pull aspect of it all.… Of course, I know enough about life to know that relationships are risky.… And for me it's about do I choose living or do I choose existing.

Windy: Yeah.

Cat: And I know that's a personal thing. I know that's not true for everyone, but that's what it is about for me.

Windy: Yeah.

Cat: And I have at least two friends I can think of who would rather exist because they're too fearful of the potential pain of getting involved with somebody else.

Windy: And are you saying at any level, 'I wish I were like them?'

Cat: No. I'm saying I'd be much more sad if I felt like them.

Windy: Right, exactly.

Cat: Or if I felt I was like them.

Windy: I'm interested in the topic of regret and what people regret. And people regret, particularly at the time of life that we're talking about that you're in at the moment, they regret more not taking action than taking action.

Cat: Yes, and I work in a hospice, so I have a lot of conversations with people at end of life talking about regrets and things, and … that's certainly my experience of talking to people.

Windy: Yeah. Since we are talking about betrayal, what stance can you take towards betrayal that doesn't stop you from pursuing the path that we've been talking about?

Cat: I think it's just about the notion of risk. I didn't give you the specifics of the examples, it didn't seem particularly important, but they were both infidelities and both unexpected. And ... [*pause*] I suppose it's the acknowledging that I can't control somebody else or somebody else's behaviour, I can only, to some extent, control my own and what I do with whatever is in front of me at any given time.

Windy: That's right.

Cat: And, so ... [*long pause*], yeah, I think betrayal is only one of the painful things that goes on in relationships. It may not even be the most painful, actually, if I think about what I now work with which is caring for people as they're dying, etc. There's lots of things on the scale of horrible parts of relationships.

Windy: Yeah. But that's part of the risk, isn't it, because you could join your other two friends and retire.

Cat: Yeah.

Windy: 'That's it, I'm retired from relationships.'

Cat: Yeah.

Windy: But you're not prepared to do that.

Cat: I don't want to do that, no. No, I don't want to do that.

Windy: Right, and that's the important thing.

Cat: I even spoke to my daughter about it quite recently because she's 15, has cut off contact from her father relatively recently, and so I feel like she absolutely relies on me as her secure base, etc. So, I just started a conversation with her. I wasn't expecting to say this, but I must've at some level have planned it, I suppose, I said to her, 'What I'd really like for my 60th birthday is a boyfriend.' I think we were driving somewhere at the time and her response was quite different from what I expected, she said, 'Well, Mum, if Dad can get a girlfriend, you can get a boyfriend.' So I said, 'OK, that's not really a compliment, but,' and then I said, 'So you wouldn't mind?' and she said, 'No!' and then she said, 'As long as I liked them,' and I thought there's the rub. But, anyway, I feel like for myself I've cleared some obvious obstacles that might have been my excuses.

Windy: Yeah. We've talked about a number of obstacles today, but we've found our way to deal with those. There may be future obstacles that you'll find, but, if you have a philosophy which says, 'When I find an obstacle, I'm gonna do my best to deal with it,' rather than, 'If I find an obstacle, I'm gonna retire with my two friends.'

[*Throughout this segment, I have helped Cat to see that there are two ways forward: Obstacle ➙ Retire from relationships or Obstacle ➙ Deal with it.*]

Cat: Yes. ... Yes. And in a way, they are a really useful indicator of where I don't want to be. If this never happens for me, and it might not, and actually I can kind of accept that because ... [*pause*] I don't want to be on my deathbed saying, 'Well, I kind of checked out about 20 years ago, or 30 years ago,' whatever. I don't want to have that as my truth.

Windy: Right, OK. So let's bring this to an end. How are you gonna summarise what we talked about and what are you gonna take away?

[*This was a little abrupt, but I felt with Cat that I could bring the session to an end in a straightforward way, without much ado.*]

Cat: ... [*Long pause*] This is no reflection on you when I say I didn't really expect to feel, I do feel something has unstuck through this conversation and I think … I'm hopeful that I might have got what I wanted from this session. I mean, the proof will be slightly in the pudding. I don't mean a relationship but noticing a shift in my approach, etc. And, so I feel lighter leaving this conversation.

Windy: Right. And that's often a good indicator. People do talk about lightness, and I think that's a good indication that something has changed.

Cat: Yeah.

Windy: And I think the way I see it is actually that you being able to take away from what we've discussed certain points that will be able to be helpful for you to keep the momentum going in the direction that you want. And I'm gonna contact you in three months with my little questionnaire which will help you to reflect on what you've achieved. So, we shall see what happens in three months.

Cat: Thank you so much. This has been really interesting. I did do a workshop with you about 18 months ago and I have also been beginning to think from my professional point of view about the interest in single-session therapy. So, it's been interesting on a number of levels.

Windy: My pleasure. All the best. Nice to meet you. Take care, bye bye.

Cat: I really wish you all the best with the book.

Cat's Follow-Up Questionnaire

Date: 23-12-24

Question	Response
1. What progress did you make on the issue that you brought to the session. Indicate the amount of progress you have made on this issue by using a 0% (no progress) – 100% (problem solved) scale.	**Issue Brought to the Session (Please name this):** Betrayal: The impact of betrayal in relationships on my ability to find a long-term partner now. **Amount of progress made:** Shift in attitude within the single session and commitment to carrying that into my approach towards meeting men via online dating. **Factors that helped me make progress:** Accepting that much was outside of my control and that I might not find what I am longing for somehow enabled me to begin to hold the issue less defensively/more open-mindedly.

	Factors that were absent that could have helped me make more progress: I don't know of any specifically.
2. Did you make any progress on other issues that you have that you did not bring to our session? Please elaborate.	I tend towards holding myself to overly high standards and this session increased my self-compassion overall.
3. How would you describe your relationship with Windy Dryden in the session?	I was aware of his warmth but also his clear boundaries and directive approach, which is key to single-session therapy. I felt very clearly seen and understood within the session by Windy.
4. What, if anything, did Windy Dryden do during the session that was helpful to you?	Close to the end of the session Windy said that he had not heard anything that made him think anything other than what I wanted was possible for me. I found that reassuring and a positive antidote to the shame I have always carried around this issue.
5. What, if anything, did Windy Dryden	Nothing. I was aware of the 'agenda' aspect of the single session model, so it necessarily did

do during the session that was unhelpful to you?	not have the organic flow of a more relational, long-term model, but I had agreed to this so it was not unhelpful to me, just unfamiliar for a therapy session, compared to the therapy I have experienced in my life.
6. How helpful did you find the pre-session form if you were sent one? Please elaborate.	Very helpful for clarifying for myself exactly what I needed to work on in the session and enabling me to come well prepared. I think it saved wasting some of the the actual session time and thus maximised its efficiency.
7. How helpful did you find the audio-recording of your session? Please elaborate.	Very helpful because I found I could not remember much detail of the session until I listened back to it carefully. It was a useful means for reflection on the session.
8. How helpful did you find the transcript of your sessions? Please elaborate.	In truth, I have not read it, which suggests that I got what I needed from the audio recording.
9. How does Single-Session Therapy compare with	It has elements of coaching and CBT in how it feels i.e., it feels more intellectual than more humanistic/relational therapy

other therapies that you have had? Please elaborate.	models. On the positive side, it felt very containing and productive as a therapy session and delivered what it had set out to deliver. Most therapy does not promise to deliver anything in one session.
10. What improvements, if any, do you think need to be made to the Single-Session Therapy framework?	I find this a difficult question to answer from my level of experience of it, i.e. beginner.
11. Please give any additional feedback that your responses to the questions above have not covered.	I found this a fascinating experience and a useful one that was directly relevant to the issue I brought. I went on a date within a few weeks of the session and was aware that I was more relaxed about the outcome than I would otherwise have been and able to take away a more positive attitude about myself.

My Reflections and Summary

On her pre-session form, Cat stated that she wanted to consider the impact of experiences of being betrayed in romantic relationships on her ability to be genuinely optimistic about the likelihood of finding a loving long-term relationship. It turned out that completing the pre-session form made Cat realise that she didn't believe she will have another good love relationship in her life, even though it is what she longs for. By the end of the session her *goal* was to have made some inroads into breaking down that barrier and be able to embody a sense of possibility ahead.

Cat seemed to have obtained what she hoped for from the session regarding this, and she was rather surprised that she did. She said that she felt lighter leaving the conversation than when she joined it, which, as I noted in the session, is often an indication that some kind of positive shift has occurred. Interestingly, we did not deal with the issue of betrayal in the session since, from Cat's perspective, it did not loom as significant an issue as she thought it would when she volunteered for the session.

On her feedback questionnaire, Cat did not use the 0–100% progress scale but said that she made a shift in attitude towards the possibility of meeting someone and made a commitment to carrying that change into her approach towards meeting men via online dating. She also noted that the session helped her overall to increase her self-compassion.

As with my work with Ruth in the previous chapter, I think I did a reasonably good job in the session with Cat, and again, I did not cover too much ground. As with my session with Ruth, I think the salient issues for Cat emerged from our conversation in a relaxed way, and I did not have to introduce any concepts from REBT into the session. I felt that I did not adequately deal with Cat's sense of self-protection, but I think we covered this in a more general way when we spoke about dealing with obstacles.

In terms of our therapeutic relationship, Cat said that she was aware of my warmth but also of my clear boundaries and directive approach, which as she said is key to single-session therapy. She said that she felt very clearly seen and understood within the session by me. Cat said that she found the following particularly helpful. Close to the end of the session, I said that I had not heard anything that made me think anything other than what Cat wanted was possible for her. She found that reassuring and a positive antidote to the shame she had always carried around this issue.

Regarding the pre-session form, recording, and transcript, Cat mentioned the following. She found the pre-session for very helpful for clarifying exactly what she needed to work on in the session and for enabling her to come well prepared. She said that it maximised the use of the session concerning the efficient use of time. Cat found the audio-recording very helpful because she found she could not remember much of the session until she listened back to it carefully. She said that it was a useful means for reflection on the session. Cat did not read the transcript as she got what she needed from the recording.

5

Dealing with Rejection

Date: 10-10-24
Time: 34 mins 25 secs

Sylvia's Pre-Session Form

Sylvia mentioned on her pre-session form that she wanted to discuss a friendship breakdown that occurred four years previously, which she continues to think about, and that has led her to feel insecure about approaching future relationships and friendships.

Her *goal* was to achieve a sense of peace and feel more capable of moving on. She addressed this issue multiple times in previous therapy, which has helped her, but she has not been able to fully move on. Sylvia said that her strengths are that she has a good sense of her 'self' and her self-worth. She considered herself a good person and was surrounded by loving family and friends.

The Session

Windy: So, from your perspective, what's the purpose of our conversation today?

Sylvia: So, I think what I wrote on the form was to help me understand and work out in my head my thoughts and feelings around this situation that happened, and that centres around rejection.

Windy: And what would you like to gain by the end of the session?

[Right at the outset, I ask Sylvia for her goal for the session]

Sylvia: More understanding, for sure. It's something I've worked on before, but I feel like there's something that still I can't quite work out, and to get a sense of feeling settled with it, like being able to move on and move away without coming back to it so often.

Windy: So, why don't you give me a context and then I'd like to find out what you have tried already to deal with the issue. But maybe we could start with the context?

[I realise that I am leading the session here. Alternatively, I could have asked Sylvia what the best way to start addressing this issue

*would be to maximise her chances of
achieving her session goal.*]

Sylvia: Sure, yeah. So, to give you a brief
background, the rejection is about the ending
of a friendship with two girls. We had been
friends for over 10 years, really. They were
my high school, classmate friends. I come
from a really small town, so, in my opinion,
it was a very small environment. So, we
really grew up together. I come from Italy.
So, when I moved to the UK, obviously
really far away, our relationship had started
changing earlier than that but it really started
changing when I moved away for a long
time. And the rejection point that I'm trying
to get to is that they ended up becoming
really, really close and I ended up feeling like
rejected, left out of this club, if you will.

Windy: So, there's a three, there's a triangle, in a
sense.

Sylvia: Yeah.

Windy: So, before that happened, how would you
describe the closeness with one another that
you and they had with each other and had
with you?

Sylvia: So, I knew one of them for a bit longer. We
were classmates in middle school as well.
And, when we went to high school, the third

one joined us. So, I introduced them to each other. And we were close, I would say kind of the same throughout high school, but I think halfway through they became a lot closer between the two of them than I was. So, I really felt like a third wheel with them.

Windy: Do you understand why that happened?

Sylvia: I'm not sure. I think maybe perhaps they clicked more. You know how some people just click or they just find each other? It was like really evident.

Windy: Did they spend more time with each other rather than you?

Sylvia: Yes.

Windy: And did you raise that as an issue at the time?

Sylvia: At the time, no because I feel like I was always a bit of a social butterfly. I had many groups of friends, but they were always the ones I would go back to. So, I wasn't bothered.

Windy: So, you had many groups of friends.

Sylvia: Yes.

Windy: And what about them, did they have many groups of friends or did they just have each other?

Sylvia: I think they mostly had each other. They still had friends, of course, but they didn't have a similar bond with anyone else, where I did have other friends.

Windy: So, you had other friends, other bonds as well. So, they really didn't. They knew other people, but they had each other and you were flying around from group to group. But you would come back to this group, but then you noticed that they were closer to each other than they were to you.

Sylvia: Yeah. I hadn't really thought about it in that way, but, yeah, you're right.

Windy: So, then what happened?

Sylvia: So, what happened is that this became really, really evident. We had a couple of fights throughout the years. Obviously, you can imagine 16, 17-year-olds. We had a big fight. Well, I had a fight with them, I suppose. They still stayed together.

Windy: So, you had a fight with both of them?

Sylvia: Yes. There was a misunderstanding.

Windy: Over what?

Sylvia: This is a whole other situation, but there was another friend that basically got between me and them. So, we separated. So, the two of them stayed together and I got separated. And then after a year or so we came back together and we ironed it out and said, 'Oh, this was a really silly misunderstanding. Why did we even do this?' and we became friends again for a fair few years after that.

Windy: And was there still the sense that they were closer to each other than you were to them?

Sylvia: Yes. By then, yes.

Windy: So, there's always that dynamic in the friendship group.

Sylvia: Yes, in the last years for sure, yeah. And I brought that up to them and I said, 'I'm not really feeling comfortable. I feel left out. I feel like we're not the same as we were before.' And they were understanding and they were like, 'I'm so sorry you felt that way.' There was very much an understanding, not, 'To make it up to you,' but, 'We're gonna try to acknowledge this and behave differently,' which didn't really happen. And it ended up being me trying to start conversations and engaging and them not being as responsive as they used to be.

Windy: So, there was a distancing between you and them.

Sylvia: Definitely.

Windy: And you tried to initiate things, but they pulled back.

Sylvia: Yes. And eventually it all came to like a close, I suppose. I think it was 2020, actually, Covid.

Windy: Are they still in Italy?

Sylvia: Yeah, they're still in Italy and I was in England.

Windy: How long had you been in England for?

Sylvia: By then six, seven years.

Windy: So, you came in 2013? 2014?

Sylvia: 2014, yeah.

Windy: OK. So, did that distance of geography increase the distance in the friendship group?

Sylvia: Yes, and that's what I originally thought. But the fact that they were also separated – they were in Italy but in two completely different bits. They also went to uni in completely different places, in completely different regions. So, I thought at that point there is no actual difference, really, so why am I being treated this way?

Windy: Well, from your perspective they may have been. From their perspective we don't know.

Sylvia: Well, I can only speak to my perspective.

Windy: Sure. So, from your perspective, it was like, 'Look, we're all separated. It can't be the geography that accounts for this.'

Sylvia: So, yeah, I think we stopped talking that year. I was reaching out for them constantly – well, not constantly perhaps – and they were not replying or not engaging.

Windy: So, when you contacted them, did you always contact them together or did you contact them separately?

Sylvia: A bit of both. Mostly together because we had a WhatsApp group.

Windy: So, you contacted them on your WhatsApp group. And, so was it sudden or a tailing off?

Sylvia: I think it was slowly changing. So that brought me to feel like these feelings of rejection. However awful they are, I think I slowly came to an understanding. I understand what went on there.

Windy: What was your understanding then?

Sylvia: My understanding was that we grew apart, sadly. I think we became different people and I think, even talking about political views or social views, I could see myself changing from what our shared mentality was then.

Windy: They were more closely aligned with each other on these issues?

Sylvia: Yeah. I would say so, yeah.

Windy: So you were changing, they weren't?

Sylvia: I'm assuming they changed as well. We just changed in different ways.

Windy: They changed more closely together and you changed away from them.

Sylvia: Yeah.

Windy: So was that your understanding of what had happened?

Sylvia: I think so and I think there was also a part of me that I think ... which makes me emotional every time, really ... I think ... [*pause*] they have done this with other girls before.

Windy: Done what?

Sylvia: ... I suppose breaking the relationship up or like rejecting them and pushing them out of the group, because we used to be four. Actually, I forgot, sorry.

Windy: There was a fourth one?

Sylvia: Sorry, yeah. Well, she wasn't as close as the three of us were.

Windy: Well, there was always four musketeers before they became three. So, when you became emotional just a minute ago, what was going through your mind that you were resonating with in terms of the emotionality?

[*Sylvia had become emotional, and I wanted to understand what she was feeling. Whenever a person becomes emotional in a single session, it signifies that something important is being experienced that needs to be understood. Prior to this comment, I allowed Sylvia plenty of time to explain the context of this issue so that I could comprehend it, and so that she could bring the issue to the forefront of her mind.*]

Sylvia: I think it's that ... [*pause*] the sense that I thought we would always be together and ... I didn't recognise the signs. Actually, I recognised when they did the same to other girls and I thought, 'Oh shoot, this wasn't what I thought.'

Windy: Right. So, you thought that the three of you would always be together, and it hasn't turned out like that.

Sylvia: Yeah. Obviously, we would talk about, 'When we're 30 we'll still be friends. We'll come to each other's weddings,' or, 'We'll meet.' I had the expectation of that friendship, that future, and it's just not.

Windy: So how have you tried to deal with your feelings up to now?

        [*Having got the context of the issue, I ask Sylvia for her past attempts to deal with the issue.*]

Sylvia: So I've spoken to other friends and done some therapy. I've talked about it in therapy before. And ... I think it took me a bit to understand my role in that, really. I think I acknowledged in the first few years I wasn't as ... responsive or available. I think I wasn't maybe as good at messaging back and stuff like that. So, I do take responsibility for that. So, I guess it was about looking at my role in this relationship. So, I do take that responsibility, but then I guess it was also looking logically, realistically at people right now. I don't think we would fit with each other anymore. And that's what I think my last bit of therapy was about, thinking would we be friends right now? I'm not sure we would.

Windy: And has that had an impact on your feelings?

Sylvia: Yeah. I feel like there was a bit of grieving there. It felt like a breakup. Actually, worse than a breakup. With other relationships I've never really … hung onto this for so long. I mean, it's been a long time now, to be fair.

Windy: Hung onto what?

Sylvia: … I suppose these feelings, these thoughts. I feel like what bothered me is that, if I think about future friendships or meeting other people, I have a little bit of a thought in my mind what if it happens again? What if there's another group of friends and I'll be rejected again or I'll be a third wheel again, I suppose? So, I think that's one of the things that doesn't click with me. Do you know what I mean?

Windy: Maybe you should ride a tandem rather than a tricycle. It seems to me that I think you haven't dealt with the rejection. That's what it sounds like to me. I think you've come to it and thought, 'Maybe I've contributed to this. Fine,' and, 'We would've drifted apart anyway.' But I don't think that has helped you deal with the rejection.

[*We are about halfway through the session, and I am becoming aware that I may need to bring more input into the conversation from my perspective. So, I suggest to Sylvia that in her previous therapy, she may have examined her contribution to the situation and the fact that they may have drifted apart anyway. However, one thing she hasn't done is confront the rejection directly, and I propose to invite Sylvia to do this, as will be seen.*]

Sylvia: … You're right, yeah. I think I can try and rationalise it.

Windy: Well, the point is what's the major emotion that you feel about this rejection?

[*I begin the discussion about rejection by asking for her major emotion about this adversity.*]

Sylvia: … I feel sad.

Windy: Yeah. I'm hearing something else, and maybe I'm right and maybe I'm wrong. It'll be interesting to see what you think of my take on it.

[*I would have preferred to have been more invitational here, saying something like, 'Would you be interested in my "take" on your feelings about being rejected by these friends?'. My view is that perhaps the reason why Sylvia hasn't been able to fully move on from the rejection is that she has not dealt with her feelings of hurt.*]

Sylvia: Please do.

Windy: I'm hearing that you feel very hurt about this.

Sylvia: Oh yes, truly.

[*Sylvia resonates with this.*]

Windy: And hurt and sadness are about somewhat different things. There are two types of hurt. Would you mind if I gave you my 'take' on hurt?

[*This has a better invitational tone.*]

Sylvia: Please, absolutely. That's why I'm here.

[*I underestimated Sylvia's desire to be offered a different perspective on rejection that may help her to move on.*]

Windy: So, there's ego hurt: the idea that this rejection reflects something about you in your own mind, suggesting that you're somehow less valuable or less worthwhile – those kinds of feelings. The other type is non-ego hurt: 'I didn't deserve this.' It's more like a sorry-for-yourself kind of hurt.

I'm curious whether you resonate with either of these, or both, and if you do, which one do you resonate with most closely?

[*I am quite pleased with the brevity and clarity of my explanation here.*]

Sylvia: I would say both. I think possibly I've felt both at different times.

Windy: Have you dealt with both: the 'poor me' type hurt and the 'less me' type hurt?

Sylvia: … [*Pause*] I'm not sure. I don't know if I truly have at this point. Do you know what I mean?

Windy: Sure.

Sylvia: I think that the ego hurt definitely has a part because that's the only time ever I wondered was there something about me.

Windy: And what do you think it was about you?

Sylvia: … [*Long pause*] I think … [*pause*] it's definitely about the quality, the worth of me. Was it not worth it to be friends with me or to try to talk about?

Windy: I think we have to be really quite careful about making a distinction between your

worth in their eyes and your worth in your
eyes.

[*Sylvia has chosen to go initially with ego
hurt, and as she elaborates upon this, she
reveals her failure to make an important
distinction, as revealed in my statement
above.*]

Sylvia: OK.

Windy: So, when we just focus on that, do you think
they're both there, both of those issues are
there? Somehow, for them you were less
important, less worthwhile to them?

Sylvia: ... [*Long pause*] If I'm following you, I think
yeah. ... [*Pause*] What you're making me
think of is, I suppose ... when I thought about
it, I think it made me less worth; it made me
wonder am I worth it myself to me? Am I not
good enough? From their side I'm thinking
was I not deserving them anymore, perhaps,
in the way they wanted to? Am I following
you right?

Windy: Another way of looking at hurt is that you're
more invested in the relationship group than
they are when it comes to you. And they're
more invested in their relationship than they
are with you. So, there's that element of them
closer together and you apart. But the true
ego hurt is really when you say, 'Now, wait

a minute, this means that I'm less worthwhile as a person.' And the way to deal with the ego hurt is to stand back and look at that and say, 'Yeah, I can understand how I come to that conclusion, but am I less valuable? Can I be valuable and still feel sorrowful that they're more invested in each other than they are with me? And it doesn't, for me, mean that I'm less worthwhile to myself.'

Sylvia: Yeah, I completely see what you mean. Yeah, for sure. That's all equivalent.

Windy: So, I think the task there is to really work on you accepting yourself, even if they have rejected you, they don't accept you. It's like saying, 'Yeah, I don't like this. This is very sad and sorrowful, but I can still accept myself.' So that's the one thing. The other thing is the non-ego hurt is not making a distinction between being in a poor situation – which we could argue that you were, the poor situation being that they're closer together than you are – and you being a poor person because you're in that poor situation.

Sylvia: I see. Yes. I see what you mean, yeah.

Windy: And the way to resolve that is to, again, stand back and question and say, 'Look, am I a poor person? Do I have to pity myself and feel sorry for myself or can I be a non-poor person who's in a poor situation?'

Sylvia: Yeah, I see.

Windy: It's still gonna be painful for you whatever it is, but it will help you to move on. And I think you're stuck because somehow you haven't got to the core of the issue, I think, from just listening to you. You've been trying to deal with important issues but not at the core of it.

Sylvia: Yeah, I see what you mean.

Windy: And the core of it is hurt.

Sylvia: … Yeah…. [*Pause*] Yeah, that makes sense.

[*Listening to the audiotape of the session, I noticed that Sylvia sighs at this point. I wish I had focused on that sigh to understand what it meant. Also, now would be a good time to have asked her to summarise my points about ego and non-ego hurt and ask how she could use these ideas going forward if the points I made resonated with her. I think I brought these two types of hurt together too much. It would have been better to have separated them out better and dealt with them more distinctly.*

Another point worth making here is that it would have been better if I had asked Sylvia to put these points into her own words and to share what she made of my 'take' on hurt.]

Windy: Now, have you ever had to deal with threats to your self-esteem before in relationships or have you had any experience of working towards self-acceptance in the face of other rejections or other situations in relationships?

[*Here, I ask about any past experiences Sylvia has had regarding rejection that we can utilise in assisting her with her current issue.*]

Sylvia: Yes. I have to say, luckily few, so I think I also had very little practice in dealing with it. So, I think possibly that's why I found such difficulty dealing with it because I had never really felt like that before. For example, even with a breakup, like a boy rejecting me for someone else, yes, it was really difficult for a while but never–

Windy: But the boy never said, 'We'll be together forever.'

Sylvia: I know.

Windy: It's that element of, 'Look, they said we would be together forever and we're not.'

Sylvia: Yes, I suppose. So, I really never had the same feeling around that.

Windy: Yeah. And maybe it's useful to think about the idea that, when people say, 'We'll be together forever,' that's their feeling of the moment. It's almost as if, because they've said it, that binds them to doing it for the rest: 'You promised to be with me forever and you're not.'

Sylvia: Yeah. No, I see what you mean. Yeah. ... It's silly because it never really hurt that much. It never brought me to question myself in the same way. Never for a moment I doubted that it was my worth. Yes, I was hurt. Of course I was. But it was never about me questioning, 'Is there something wrong?'

Windy: With other breakups, you mean?

Sylvia: Yeah.

Windy: So, what is it, do you think, about this relationship that did lead you to question your worth?

Sylvia: ... I think, and I thought about it really just in preparation for this meeting, actually, just a small epiphany, I think it's because in my head I gave them so much power. I, eventually, put them on a pedestal, I think, 'Oh, they're such good friends to me. They've helped me so much.' And ... I trusted their judgement a lot. So, I think, when they rejected me, I trusted their judgement then too.

Windy: Right, yeah. 'Because I trust their judgement, if they reject me, they must be right about me.'

Sylvia: Which is insane, thinking about it when you're saying it out loud. Of course, I know it's not, but that's what I have thought.

Windy: So now you've expressed it, now you've heard yourself say it, how would you change that?

Sylvia: … I could change that thinking that whatever they think, they're still allowed to have their own opinions, even if they do think less of me. It still doesn't mean it's true.

Windy: Right. 'And I can take them off the pedestal.'

Sylvia: Yes, definitely.

Windy: 'Cos your pedestal, you look up to people rather than look across at people.

Sylvia: Yeah, and that's not a friendship.

Windy: No, that's right. I've got a phrase which I sometimes use, which is relevant here: pedestals are for statues, not people.

Sylvia: Yeah, truly.

[*I am pleased that Sylvia brought the issue of power and pedestals into our conversation, and her voicing this insight can dilute its power to affect her.*]

Windy: So maybe part of it is to recognise that, even though they were important to you, you invested them in power that they didn't have.

Sylvia: Yeah, completely.

Windy: And then you took the power that they didn't have and you used it to define yourself in ways that has stopped you from moving on, I think.

Sylvia: Yeah, in ways that actually they had never said. Those are all judgements off of my imagination.

Windy: Yeah, that's right. I think, with the breakup with guys, I don't think you invested by giving them that power.

Sylvia: No, not at all.

Windy: Exactly.

Sylvia: Yeah.

Windy: So, I think what you've mistaken is importance with power. 'Because they're important to me, I'm gonna give them the power to define me,' as opposed to, 'Yeah, they're important to me, but I'm not gonna give them that power to define me.'

Sylvia: Yeah, I agree. And, to take it one step further, I think before it all deteriorated, I had already started disagreeing and distancing. When I say distancing, I really mean maybe not blindly trusting that judgement. And I think that's why they also stepped back. I think they enjoyed having that power.

Windy: Maybe, yeah.

Sylvia: Because, if I reflect on the other girl, that's very similar to what happened: it no longer suited them or it no longer suited their standards or whatever. It became not OK, no longer acceptable. So, I think when I started becoming a bit more opinionated, a bit more me, growing up, I think that didn't suit them quite as much as before.

Windy: Dracula only gets his power by drinking the blood of other people. And there's something leech-like about your description of these people. They may have their power by thinking that they can drain other people of theirs.

Sylvia: I think there's an aspect of that, for sure. I mean, I'm not trying to make them to be like horrible.

Windy: No. I'm being a bit dramatic in my analogy.

[*Our discussion has moved on from dealing with hurt to putting her friends on a pedestal and investing them with the power that they don't have, and the possibility that her friends enjoyed having such power. My Dracula analogy was dramatic, but it seemed to fit what Sylvia was saying. The reason that Sylvia was not as affected by rejection from boyfriends was that she neither put them on pedestals nor gave them power that they did not have.*]

Sylvia: Yeah, but it helps to just get the picture. I think, when I realised that, it didn't suit them as well, I suppose.

Windy: Right, OK.

Sylvia: So that's just a different aspect of it, I think.

Windy: So, part of this is going to be, I guess, if you need to, you working towards recognising that you have the power to view yourself, they don't. That it is painful to be rejected by people who are important to you, and you've lost that so there is sadness and sorrow involved, but you're a person who's in a poor situation, not a poor person, and you can define yourself as you did in other relationships. And, if you did that, I would be very interested to see whether you can move on from this.

[I could have held off from making this summary until Sylvia had provided hers (see below).]

Sylvia: I see, yeah. I think it's really helpful to separate my judgement and understanding of the situation doesn't equal … my judgement of myself. That 'poor situation/poor me' I think makes a lot of sense as well.

Windy: Yeah, 'cos I think there are those two different aspects of hurt that people struggle with. But I think the reason that you haven't dealt with it – I often think about in therapy sometimes we're aiming the arrow and we hit the board but we're not in the centre; we're hitting the things around. And I think you were saying, 'Well, maybe I contributed to that. Yes, fine. Maybe we've moved apart and we've grown away. Yes, that's fine,' but it didn't deal with the hurt.

Sylvia: That's exactly what I meant. There was something that I wasn't quite getting. I think you're right, that was the bit. I kept going around trying to get it but not quite, not at the centre.

Windy: So why don't you summarise what we've done from your perspective and then what you're gonna take away.

Sylvia: To summarise, I've given you the background, I've given you my understanding of the situation, you've given me what your understanding was after what I told you. And there, I think, the main takeaways for me which is to actually understand, I mean there were already bits I had understood and made my peace with, I suppose, but there were bits of that situation that I hadn't understood or considered yet, which is the hurt of it and actually separating the types of hurt. I think that's brilliant and just working it out in my head is more helpful. I think also the separating my understanding of the situation: that poor situation doesn't equal poor me. The same thing with the ego hurt. I think that's really helpful to get just a different perspective on it.

Windy: And I would add just one additional point: don't give people who are important to you power that they don't have.

[*I have found it helpful to add to a person's summary an important point that they omitted.*]

Sylvia: Yes, truly.

Windy: Great. I hope you found this useful.

Sylvia: Absolutely. Thank you very much.

Windy: I'll write to you in three months on the questionnaire to see how you're getting on, OK?

Sylvia: OK. Thank you so, so much.

Sylvia's Follow-Up Questionnaire

Date: 12.12.24

Question	**Response**
1. What progress did you make on the issue that you brought to the session. Indicate the amount of progress you have made on this issue by using a 0% (no progress) – 100% (problem solved) scale.	**Issue Brought to the Session (Please name this):** Rejection **Amount of progress made:** 80% **Factors that helped me make progress:** Breaking down the issue, recognising the different types of hurt I was experiencing.

	Factors that were absent that could have helped me make more progress: More time for reflection, further processing.
2. Did you make any progress on other issues that you have that you did not bring to our session? Please elaborate.	This session helped me look at other times I felt rejected, but more specifically times that I experienced 'hurt'. It made me look at those experiences with enhanced understanding.
3. How would you describe your relationship with Windy Dryden in the session?	I felt it was easy to work with Windy, having a shared goal and under-standing of the process helped me feel like we were working together towards an outcome/resolution.
4. What, if anything, did Windy Dryden do during the session that was helpful to you?	He explained things clearly and concisely.

5. What, if anything, did Windy Dryden do during the session that was unhelpful to you?	N/a
6. How helpful did you find the pre-session form if you were sent one? Please elaborate.	It was helpful to know what to expect from the session.
7. How helpful did you find the audio-recording of your session? Please elaborate.	I do not personally find the audio helpful, I much prefer using a transcript, since it allows me to extrapolate and highlight quickly some poignant sentences or text that otherwise I might miss while listening. I personally feel like seeing things written down makes some concepts 'sink in' more.
8. How helpful did you find the transcript of your sessions? Please elaborate.	The transcript was very helpful – see above.

9. How does Single-Session Therapy compare with other therapies that you have had? Please elaborate.	Felt more direct and specific. I personally enjoyed a lot the psychoeducation element of it.
10. What improvements, if any, do you think need to be made to the Single-Session Therapy framework?	Not sure – I think Single-Session Therapy delivers what it advertises.
11. Please give any additional feedback that your responses to the questions above have not covered.	N/a

My Reflections and Summary

On her pre-session form, Sylvia stated that she wanted to consider the breaking down of a friendship in the session. This had happened four years ago and at the time of the session it still impacted how Sylvia approaches future relationships and friendships leading her to feel insecure.

Sylvia's *goal* from the session was to achieve a sense of peace and feeling more able to move on.

On her follow-up questionnaire, Sylvia rated her progress on the 0–100% scale at 80%. She said that what was helpful about the session was that it helped her to break down the issue, recognising the different types of hurt she was experiencing. Sylvia also said that the session helped her look at other times she felt rejected, but more specifically times that she experienced 'hurt'. She was able to view these experiences with greater understanding.

I was pleased with my work with Sylvia. I took my time to understand the context of the problem and discovered what she did in the past to deal with the problem. Although Sylvia had derived some benefit from discussing the issue in therapy before – doing so helped her to consider her contribution to the friendship breakdown and the fact that they may have drifted apart anyway, she had not dealt in a focused way with the rejection and the hurt she experienced. This became a major focus, and I was able to offer Sylvia my REBT-informed 'take' on the issue. However, it would have been better if I had separated out ego hurt from poor me hurt and had asked Sylvia to summarise her understanding of these concepts and their likely helpfulness to her. This tallies with what Sylvia said on her feedback form. She wanted more time for reflection and further processing.

In terms of our therapeutic relationship, Sylvia said she felt it was easy to work with me and, having a shared goal and understanding of the process helped her feel like we were working together towards an outcome/resolution. She referenced my clear and concise explanations as being particularly helpful.

Regarding the pre-session form, recording, and transcript, Sylvia mentioned the following. She found the pre-session form useful as it helped her to know what to expect from the session. She did find the audio helpful, much preferring to use the transcript, since it allowed her to extrapolate and highlight quickly some poignant sentences or text that otherwise she might have missed while listening. Sylvia said that for her seeing things written down makes some concepts 'sink in' more.

6

Dealing with Self-Doubt and Fear of Failure

Date: 28/01/25
Time: 41 mins 57 secs

Louise's Pre-Session Form

Louise's mentioned on her pre-session form that she feels stuck with feelings of self-doubt with academic failure and situations where she has fear of failure. Her *goal* in seeking a session with me was to identify the underlying reasons and breaking the cycle. She had previously addressed the issue of self-doubt through meditation, yoga and breathwork. She listed as her strengths resilience and being open to working on herself.

The Session

Windy: So, from your perspective, what's the purpose of our conversation today?

Louise: For feeling stuck, really, in a few areas of my life and not feeling that I can move forward.

Windy: And the goal would be for you?

Louise: Well, the two issues are: one, I'm training to be a counsellor and I seem to procrastinate a lot. I'm OK during the sessions, everything's going well with the clients, but it's the academic stuff. I find it really difficult to actually put stuff on paper, so I end up leaving everything to the last minute.

Windy: And then what happens?

Louise: And then I do it at the last minute, but it's all a rush and everything's last minute.

Windy: And do they get graded?

Louise: OK so far because I manage to do it at the last minute.... It's not that I'm not organised, because I try to find the time, but then I always end up doing everything else before it. So I'll sit down, get everything organised and then I'll look over and think, 'Oh, I'll

start cooking. I'll walk the dog again,' and I
put it off.

Windy: The poor dog's exhausted.

Louise: Yes. I'll do everything. I'll pick a paintbrush
up.

Windy: Yeah. Does that work in reverse? If you had
to do the painting, would you put that off and
do the academic work first?

Louise: … Not as much. It seems like it's got a whole
lot worse with the academic stuff.

Windy: OK, so where's the best place to start then,
for you?

Louise: … Sorry, what do you mean?

Windy: Well, if I'm going to help you to get unstuck,
where's the best place we're gonna start?

               [*Asking a person where is the best place to
               start sends a message that they can lead take
               the reins of the session.*]

Louise: … I guess knowing why I avoid it so much
and why … I'm doing what I'm doing; I'm
procrastinating so much.

Windy: What are your hypotheses?

[*Again, I start with the person's perspective.*]

Louise: … I think I'm scared, I always think that I'm going to get my stuff returned or my work. I think it goes back to childhood at school.

Windy: And, if you got it returned, what?

Louise: … [*Long pause*] It would be a really awful feeling, yeah.

Windy: What would that feeling indicate?

Louise: Getting it wrong…. Failure.

Windy: What would be a failure?

Louise: The work that I'd submitted.

Windy: OK. And why would that be bad?

Louise: … I just hate getting things wrong. It leaves me really feeling uncomfortable.

Windy: Right. So let me tell you a story about a student of mine years ago. I used to run a course at the University of Aston and this guy, he had taken seven years for his first degree. And I interviewed him and he said, 'There's one thing that you should know about me.' I said, 'What's that?' He said, 'Whatever I do, the first time I do it I fail.' I said, 'OK, and then what do you do?' He said, 'Well, I have a look at what I failed at, I learn from it and I do it again.' I said, 'OK.' And I said, 'What do you think that means about you?' He said, 'Well, I'm obviously not as bright as I wanna be, but I just accept the fact.' And, guess what, he failed my diploma, par for the course. But he actually made it to a quite lofty position in the field of counselling.

[*I don't often lead with a story to demonstrate a point so early in the session – and it would have been better if I had first asked Louise if she would be interested in the story, before telling it.*]

Louise: That's great, yeah.

Windy: So, what can you learn from him?

Louise: Yeah, to persevere. I mean, it doesn't matter, does it, if you don't succeed. The strange thing is I am such an advocate for that with my three children. They've all grown, they're young adults now, they're all successful and they all don't seem to have any big issues. They're really well rounded, and that's because I've always accepted them for who they are and always encouraged them to do the best they can.

Windy: And when they fail something?

Louise: If they fail, it's about how you get over it.

Windy: Right. So, there you go. So, a combination of learning from my ex-student and a combination of learning from somebody called Louise. About you learning from yourself. In order to learn you've got to put this into practice.

Louise: Yeah

Windy: Now, what are you procrastinating on at the moment?

[Having established she can learn from my ex-student and from myself, I ask about a current example of the issue.]

Louise: At the moment, I've got to do a theory on person-centred counselling, which is fine and there's lots of stuff that I can do. And I've written a rough. I've not put it together. And then I've got to … *[pause]* put some work together on depression and antidepressants, but my part is to do new types of antidepressants, as in MDMR and psilocybin, which is really interesting.

Windy: OK. So which task shall we look at in terms of procrastination that you predict that you're going to bring to the table?

Louise: Well, I don't know what this block is that I've got ... because I know, if I submit it and it's not acceptable, I can do it again. I get this awful feeling of this dread and it's so uncomfortable.

Windy: What do you do with the dread?

Louise: ...   [*Long pause*] Well, I know the dread's there but I'm running from the dread and I'm not sitting with the dread.

Windy: OK. So, two things: what do you dread at that point?

Louise: ... [*Pause*] I suppose I'm dreading if the outcome is bad.

Windy: Right. OK, so let's plug in insights from ex-student and from Louise. How are you going to respond to that dread? So, there you are, you sit down and you're feeling dread. Now what?

Louise: ... I need to just do it, submit it.

Windy: Yeah, I know, but in terms of what you need to remind yourself of on that point. In other words, you can respond to dread by actually walking away from it, which sounds like what you've been doing; or you could learn from the ex-student and from yourself. What I'm saying is, if you learn from my ex-student and from yourself, what would that sound like? So, dread and then what?

Louise: … [*Pause*] Dread and … acceptance?

Windy: Acceptance of what?

Louise: Acceptance of trusting the outcome.

Windy: And, if you fail, what?

Louise: … I'll do it again.

Windy: Right. And that means what about you?

Louise: … [*Pause*] It means that I've got to go forward, yeah.

Windy: Yeah. Does it mean you're a failure?

Louise: No, it means I'm resilient and brave and all of those things.

Windy: Yeah, like my student. He just said, 'Well, look, I'm not as bright as I'd like to be.' I'm not suggesting that that's the case in your case, but I'm just saying he wasn't daunted and he never procrastinated. That's the other thing. He said, 'Look, when I sit down, I know I'm going to fail, chances are, but I can only learn from my failure by doing it and actually failing and getting the information back.'

So, the other thing is it's about you accepting the dread. You can run away from dread or you can sit down with dread. Have you ever sat down with dread and worked at all or have you always run away from it?

Louise: No. I mean, I would actually say that I'm a really resilient person as in … things that have happened in my life and I've sat through them and I've been through them and not run away.

Windy: Right. So that's the bit that you wanna bring to this task, the bit of you that's resilient, the bit of you that can actually sit down and tolerate the dread, because chances are for a while the dread's gonna come up. So it's like a process: you sit down, you feel dread, you have a choice – you can either walk away from dread, walk the dog again, do the painting or whatever it is, or you could sit down there, accept the dread, bring in the special resilience, bring to the space the person that can learn from failure, bring to the situation the point that is that failure is not going to define you. That's your choice.

[*Here, I am drawing on Louise's strengths – her resilience and making the point that she has a choice when it comes to responding to dread – to face it and sit with it resiliently or to walk away from it.*]

Louise:　Yeah.

Windy:　And I'm inviting you to do something which goes against the grain. Do you know why?

Louise:　Yeah.

Windy:　Why?

Louise:　'Cos things are not gonna change, are they, otherwise.

Windy:　No. If you go with the grain, you walk away from the dread.

Louise:　Yeah.

Windy:　Change is about going against the grain on this situation. There's no magic. It would be nice if I could wave this magic wand and you don't experience the dread. But I'm saying you can incorporate the dread into the process.

Louise:　Yeah.

Windy:　Louise sits down, feels dread, decides to stay there with resilience, prepared to learn from any failure that she's experienced and shows herself the same conditions as she shows her children.

Louise:　Yeah.

Windy: And then, the more you practise that, the more that becomes the norm.

Louise: Yeah.

Windy: Because you've been practising procrastination.

Louise: It's almost like a habit.

Windy: It is, yeah. Incidentally, you don't need any more practice at that. You're not saying, 'Professor Dryden, can you teach me how to procrastinate?' You don't need that. So, when you think about it like that, that you have a choice: you could either do what you normally do or you could actually go against the grain and actually bring to the table your own strengths and your own resilience and your own different attitude towards failure and bringing yourself up. Can you see yourself doing the second? Can you picture yourself doing that?

Louise: Doing the second?

Windy: The second, yeah, which is to stay with the dread and then going forward.

Louise: Yeah. I'm going to really try because I've got until July and then I finish. So, I can't walk away. I've got to do this.

Windy: Do you know you used the 'T' word?

Louise: ... The 'T' word?

Windy: The 'T' word.

Louise: What's the 'T' word?

Windy: Well, we've got the 'F' word, which you didn't use, which is good, but you used the 'T' word. I've got something here with the 'T' word. I want you to read it out for me, please?

Louise: 'Do or do not. There is no try.' Simple.

               [*This is the famous quote of Yoda from Star Wars.*]

Windy: That's the 'T' word – try. So, I don't accept contracts to try. I accept contracts to either do or do not.

Louise: Yeah.

Windy: Because, if you try, you only try rather than do.

Louise: Yeah.

Windy: So that's something else to bear in mind. Now, if you can imagine doing that and then sit down and do it, the most important thing is I think I would add is have a specific time to start work, because then you know one minute after that you've started to procrastinate.

Louise: Yeah. Set some goals with time limits, like an hour, then a break.

Windy: And then do these other tasks that you've been doing before the work, do it after the work, if you want to. Now, what's the other area you're stuck in?

[*It would be better if I had asked Louise if there anything else she wanted to say about the procrastination issue before moving on to the second issue.*]

Louise: That I feel stuck in. So, I've been in a relationship with my partner for 15 years and we don't live together because I was raising my children and I just felt that it was best that he didn't move in. I wanted to raise them, I didn't want another man coming in and trying to replace their father, really. It's worked as it is. We've broken up twice, but there's no big dramas in our relationship. He's a really good man. I love him. I definitely want to be with him. But he's really keen for us to move in together. He's got his own house, I've got my house. We're very independent. And it works really nicely. He comes and stays here once or twice a week and sometimes I'll stay at his. We go on holiday. He gets on well with my children.

One of my children is now living in America, the other two, they're 21 and 24, so they're busy working. So, I've actually got a lot more time now to invest in the relationship, whereas before everything was about the children. And, financially, it would be the sensible thing to do as well, because it's quite a struggle for me, keeping the house going. But I just have this, I don't know if it's because I've got so used to being independent and having my own space or whether I'm stuck. That's what's been going on in my mind: am I stuck? Because, actually, he's been staying here for the last week because he's getting some building work done on his house, and it's been so lovely. And the children have said, when they've got in from work, as well, just having a man around to help as well.

Windy: So, what if the next time you see him he says to you, 'You know, Louise, I've been thinking, I think that we're fine just the way we are. I think we should continue our relationship you living where you live, I live where I live, I can come for a week, you can come to me for a week, but let's move forward on that basis'? How would you feel?

Louise: I think I'd actually… it would really make me want to move in with him.

Windy: Oh really? Why's that?

Louise: I wanna move forward. I do. My life could be easier and richer.

Windy: Alright. And what about then, instead of him saying that, he comes to you and he says, 'You know what, Louise, that time that I spent with you was great with the kids. Let's stop faffing around. Let's move in together,' how would you react?

Louise: Well, that's actually what he's saying.

Windy: Right, and how are you reacting?

Louise: Yeah, we're semi looking at places. I haven't put my house on the market yet.

Windy: How can you semi look? You look at half a house and then say, 'Oh, I've seen enough. I'll look at the other half later'?

Louise: What I mean is he's sent me a few houses that could be potentials.

Windy: When I put the first scenario when he says, 'Well, let's stay the way we are,' it sounds like you were saying, 'No, let's move in together.' The energy seemed to be flowing. Now, what I'm saying is what's your reaction and what's your feeling if he were to say, 'Come on, let's stop faffing around, let's move in together'?

Louise: Yeah. There is this tiny bit of resistance, and I don't know if it's because, like I said, I've been on my own for so long. You know when you're younger, you just go and do things and you're a bit braver and you just dive in. I mean, it's been 15 years. I don't know if I'm just being really wary.

Windy: What happened to that little bit of resistance when I put the first scenario to you?

Louise: What happened to it?

Windy: Yeah.

Louise: ... It disappeared.

Windy: Well, how do you understand that, then? What sense do you make of that?

Louise: ... [*Pause*] I don't know.

Windy: What I'm hearing, and I don't know whether it means anything to you, but are you interested in my reaction to that?

Louise: ... Yeah, definitely.

Windy: In the first scenario, when he said, 'Let's leave things as we are,' you brought to that your reaction, 'No' – autonomy – 'No, let's move in.' So, you're not the recipient of anything. You made a choice in reaction to him pulling away. But, when he comes to you and says, 'Let's do it,' there's a part of you that's, again, almost like keeping some independence and autonomy in saying, 'No.' I don't know if that means anything to you, but that's what it seemed like to me.

Louise: Yeah. So, you think … [*pause*] that's what I'm resisting?

Windy: I don't know. If it means something to you, that's fine. If it doesn't mean anything to you, then we can throw it out.

Louise: Yeah. It's interesting, though, when you say, if he was to change his mind about it, I still want it. So, I guess I do still want it. I just feel a bit scared, I suppose.

[*My 'autonomy' hypothesis was not confirmed by Louise. Instead, she thought she was resisting failure – this time in a relationship context.*]

Windy: Of what?

Louise: … Maybe I'm scared of failing again. I've got this sense of, I spoke to you about my fear of failure, well the relationship I had for

18 years with my children's dad, that failed, and that really hurt me that it failed.

Windy: When you say 'it failed', what does that mean?

Louise: To me it seemed like it failed, because I always wanted that family. I wanted mum and dad to bring up the children.

Windy: Well, you did, didn't you?

Louise: I did, but it wasn't a complete family.

Windy: Well, how do you mean?

Louise: Well, Dad wasn't living here.

Windy: He left after how long?

Louise: Well, we was together for 18 years, but ... the children were young.

Windy: And what's your perspective of why the relationship, and I'll use your terminology, 'failed'?

Louise: ... [*Pause*] It failed because he was ... having an affair and he was gambling. There was a lot of lies and distress.

Windy: And this new one is also a lothario and a gambler, is he?

Louise: No. He's the complete opposite.

Windy: OK. Well, there's a guarantee how you can avoid failure, is to avoid success.

Louise: … Yes.… I guess it's the same context of what you said before about trying and giving it a go.

          [*Louise is generalising from the first issue we discussed to this one. I am always encouraged when a person does this.*]

Windy: Yeah, and I'm sure you bring two people together they're gonna have some conflicts, but you can actually work it through, can't you?

Louise: Yeah.

Windy: How long have you been with this guy?

Louise: Almost 15 years.

Windy: And have you had conflicts with him?

Louise: We've had conflicts, yeah.

Windy: Yeah, you've broken up a couple of times, haven't you?

Louise: Yeah.

Windy: Why did you break up?

Louise: Well, actually the first one, I'm actually really trusting but he had trust issues because his first marriage failed because his wife was having an affair.

Windy: Not with your husband, I hope.

Louise: Not with my husband. And for a long time he sensed it. And, obviously, he thought he was going mad and then it came out. He had a mistrust of women, actually. So, when we met, he found it very hard to trust. And he really trusts now. We've got a very good, solid relationship there. So, I've taught him, I guess, to trust and he's taught me a lot. He's taught me to slow down. I used to have lots of jobs and I was quite frantic and doing lots of different things all at once, and he slowed me down. So we've helped each other.

He's very good for me.... I mean, we broke up because, actually ... at the time ... [*pause*] he couldn't understand that my children came first, because they were young children at the time and young teenagers, and he felt that I didn't give him enough time, which there's a part of that that I own because I was very 100% everything was about the children. And then Mum and Dad was getting really old and they was ill, so I was looking after them. There was a lot of things going on and I was juggling a lot, and he felt that he just came way down the list, which I think he did.

But life's moved on now and we're in different positions. I'm 54, he's 56, our children are grown up. Sadly, our parents aren't with us any more.

Windy: So, it sounds like you have the time and opportunity to put one another first.

Louise: Yeah.

Windy: And, if you did move in, do you think you would be able to maintain a sense of independence and autonomy?

Louise: Yes, I do, actually, because through me doing this course, I was a people pleaser before and I didn't like to say no, and I've become a lot stronger with my autonomy. So, I'm able to say no now. And he's independent and I'm independent. We've got lots of friends and we do things separate; we're not totally immersed and dependent on each other.

Windy: If you were to make that commitment, which house would you live in?

Louise: Well, we're both selling houses and then buying another house joint.

Windy: And marriage?

Louise: Yeah, well, he did actually propose to me, but he proposed to me three years ago. My dad was really ill at the time and then my mum got ill a year after. So, there's been quite a lot of bereavements. So, it just hasn't felt the right time. But, yeah, we speak about it. I said maybe next year. It's a strange thing at this age, though, because marriage is not high on my agenda.

Windy: No. Is it high on his?

Louise: … He's quite romantic, actually. He likes the idea of us just celebrating our love for one another. But, actually, he has said to me, 'If you don't want to get married, we're together, we're committed.' I think he's quite flexible, but I think he'd like to celebrate what we have. But, for me, financially, I just think it's another expense and I don't think it really means that much to me, the more I think about it. It would have if he shared the children with me for that purpose. But I don't know, at my grand old age … it doesn't mean-

Windy: So where do you feel stuck, then?

Louise: … I sort of feel stuck that I'm not moving forward with the relationship.

Windy: And you want to move forward with the relationship?

Louise: ... He's been wanting us to move in for quite a while and obviously he's mentioned the marriage. I just ... [*long pause*] haven't made any effort to move forward.

Windy: But you haven't answered my question.

Louise: That's where I was stuck, yeah.

Windy: I'm saying do you want to move forward with the relationship?

Louise: Yeah.

Windy: So what would moving forward mean to you? Not to him, to you?

Louise: ... I suppose building a life together... as in living together. Yeah. But there is a part of me that really quite likes that he's got his home and I've got mine, because ... we don't have any big dramas. We don't seem to argue. And is that because we've got our separate homes?

Windy: Right. But, when I put the scenario where he says that, then you want to move in.

Louise: Yeah.

Windy: So, it's almost like, 'If I'm in charge, then that's fine, and it sounds like we're good as we are. When he says we're good as we are, no, I want to move in.'

Louise: Yeah.

Windy: Because, if he was to say, 'We're good as we are,' how would you view that, that is different from when you say, 'We're good as we are'?

Louise: It definitely is.

Windy: What's the difference in your mind, do you think?

Louise: ... Me calling the shots.

Windy: Right.

Louise: ... Me being in control.

Windy: Right. So, when he's calling the shots, you say, 'No, we'll do it my way.'

Louise: Yeah. I didn't say no but I've not pushed it along.

Windy: No, and I think that's part of you calling the shots.

[*Maybe there is something to my autonomy hypothesis, after all.*]

Louise: Yeah.

Windy: Now, what about the concept of, 'We call the shots'? Not, 'He calls the shots,' or, 'I call the shots,' 'We call the shots.'

Louise: Yeah.

Windy: What would that sound like?

Louise: Sounds a lot more comfortable.

Windy: So I think that's your task, because it sounds like there is love there, but I think in your mind there's an 'I' and there's a 'him', and the thing that you have to grow is this little plant called 'we'.

                [*In listening to Louise, it seemed to me that she was not using relationship language.*]

Louise: Yeah.

Windy: Let's see what the 'we' sounds like or looks like when you grow it.

Louise: Yeah. That sounds good. That's true.

Windy: If you look at it like that, what happens to the stuckness?

Louise: Yeah, I can work with that a lot more.

Windy: Yeah. So maybe that's the thing to do. In the first case with the work, you stay with the dread, you don't have to avoid it. You can actually bring to the table your strengths, which is the resilience and the thing that you used to say to your kids. With this relationship thing it's a different type of strength. It's not an intrapersonal strength, it's an interpersonal strength: 'What are 'we' going to create?'

Louise: Yeah.

Windy: And, if you water that plant, it'll be interesting to see what happens to the stuckness in that area.

Louise: ... Yeah, that makes sense. And it's just reframing it because, when you said that about how I would feel if all of a sudden he turned round and said, 'Do you know what, you stay there and I stay here,' I definitely would resist that. I've never thought of that before because it's always been him leading, him driving.

Windy: You see, part of stuckness for me is that you don't experiment with different ways of looking at things.

Louise: Yeah.

Windy: You keep doing the same things again and again and getting the same results. Whereas, what I'm doing in each of these cases is actually bringing a different perspective to it, and say, yeah, the choice is that you can respond to dread by walking away or you can respond to dread by staying there with your resilience and really show yourself that, 'If the worst happens and I fail, I'll do it again,' and all the rest of it. Now, with this one it's about widening the perspective to include the both of you, 'cos you are in a relationship together.

Louise: Yeah.... And ... at the end of the day, when I think about it, even friends and family say to me, because I do struggle sometimes financially and doing everything on my own, and they say, 'Why would you not want to move in together because you get on so well together?' We like the same things and we can help each other. There he is running a home on his own, I'm running a home on my own and, if it doesn't work, what's the worst that can happen? It doesn't work.

Windy: No. And don't forget Elizabeth Taylor got divorced how many times?

Louise: ... [*Pause*] It was quite a lot, yeah.

Windy: Six or seven.

Louise: I'm no Liz Taylor.

Windy: Right. The other thing is, when you do this academic task, you're prepared for failure but you may succeed, and the same thing here. You may go and live with him, it may not work out or it might.

Louise: Yeah.

Windy: I can answer that question. I'm going to answer it for you. Enough of this counselling nonsense. We're gonna bring to the table some real science.

Louise: What's this?

Windy: It's my crystal ball.

[*Some humour.*]

Louise: I wish.

Windy: This is going back to Amazon, actually. It doesn't work. They sold it to me under false pretences.

Louise: Wouldn't that be great.

Windy: We're coming to the end of our session now. Do you want to go over what you're gonna take away from our conversation?

Louise: Yeah.... I'm not gonna walk away from the dread. I'm not going to. I'm gonna face it and look at my resilience and just do it.

Windy: There'll still be a part of you that wants to walk the dog.

Louise: Always.

Windy: But you don't have to act on that part until afterwards.

Louise: Yeah. And you always feel so much better after, don't you, when you've completed something or you've broken that cycle.

Windy: Yeah, but that doesn't help you because you've still got to deal with the dread. And that's what you're saying. Your job is to recognise that with dread you can walk away from it, you can stay with it resiliently and then move on.

Louise: Yeah. I'm gonna do that. I really am.

Windy: And with your relationship?

Louise: The relationship, I'm gonna water – I really like that.

Windy: Water the?

Louise: Water the 'we'/'us'.

Windy: Water the 'we'.

Louise: And, yeah, that really impacted me, what you said, actually, about if he was to come to me. That fills me with a sense of fear. So that's really help me reframe it, because it's made me realise that I do want it, actually. This is just me being resistant and stuck and scared of going forward, I think.

Windy: I don't like the term resistance. The reason I don't like it is because it hides the truth. There is a part of you that is scared and that part of you needs attention and needs looking at and needs reassuring. Calling it resistance, I don't like that term in therapy: the patient was resistant. I don't like that. Even though I've written a book on it many years ago, I've changed my mind on that subject.

Louise: Did you?

Windy: Yeah. So, it'll be interesting to see. What I'll do is to send you the recording, then the transcript later on, and then a little while down the line, two months' time send you a form to fill out to see what the outcome was, what you made of the session. And then, when I send you that, I'll ask you what name you want. I can see it now: Elizabeth Taylor.

Louise: Yes. My pseudo name.

Windy: Yeah. You can call yourself Liz.

Louise: Thank you, Windy.

Louise's Follow-up Questionnaire

Date: 01/04/25

Question	Response
1. What progress did you make on the issue that you brought to the session. Indicate the amount of progress you have made on this issue by using a 0% (no progress) – 100% (problem solved) scale.	**Issue Brought to the Session (Please name this):** **Amount of progress made:** 75% **Factors that helped me make progress:** Looking at the issues that I felt stuck with, and reframing them as if the decision was taken out of my control **Factors that were absent that could have helped me make more progress:** Maybe more time to explore history of subject

2. Did you make any progress on other issues that you have that you did not bring to our session? Please elaborate.	No
3. How would you describe your relationship with Windy Dryden in the session?	Excellent. Windy has a lovely relaxed personality that instantly helps to make others feel relaxed, I enjoyed the way he explained certain thoughts
4. What, if anything, did Windy Dryden do during the session that was helpful to you?	Windy helped me look at my situation through a different lens
5. What, if anything, did Windy Dryden do during the session that was unhelpful to you?	Nothing
7. How helpful did you find the audio-recording of your session? Please elaborate.	I feel the recording was very helpful, as there were parts I had forgotten

8. How helpful did you find the transcript of your sessions? Please elaborate.	Once again, helpful to see how session flowed
9. How does Single-Session Therapy compare with other therapies that you have had? Please elaborate.	I feel it's beneficial if there's no other issues to work on that Would need exploring, for me it was helpful as I had already had lots of counselling to move me forward with childhood issues, and this was just a feeling of being stuck in a relationship and studies
10. What improvements, if any, do you think need to be made to the Single-Session Therapy framework?	None
11. Please give any additional feedback that your responses to the questions above have not covered.	None

My Reflections and Summary

On her pre-session form, Louise stated that she wanted to understand her self-doubt and fear of failure and break the cycle she had got into. We discussed two contexts where these issues showed up – procrastinating on her studies and not committing to her relationship where the two of them would sell their houses and buy a jointly owned house. On the 0–100% progress scale, Louise said that she had made 75% progress. She said that what was helpful was looking at the issues that she felt stuck with through a different lens that I helped to provide.

I think I did a good job in the session and covered both issues well. I particularly like the links I made between the two issues. It would have been better if I had asked Louise if there was more we could have done on the first issue before unilaterally deciding to move onto the second.

In terms of our therapeutic relationship, Louise said that we had an excellent relationship. She said that I have a lovely, relaxed personality that instantly helped to make her feel relaxed. She said also that she enjoyed the way I explained certain thoughts

She found the recording helpful as there were parts of the session that she had forgotten, and the transcript was useful in helping her to see how the session flowed.

The only factor Louise said was missing that may have been helpful to her was maybe more time to explore the history of the subject.

7

Dealing with Co-dependency

Date: *28/01/25*
Time: *48 mins 0 secs*

Lily's Pre-Session Form

Lily mentioned on her pre-session form that she wanted to discuss a a strong pattern in her romantic relationships. She leaps into serious relationships with people who are very fragile or unavailable and who lack emotional intelligence and resilience. She tends to idealise these people and are drawn to their mystery and intrigue and falls madly in love. Once she decides to end the relationship, she says it's like a spell is broken and she gets resentful of herself and her ex-partners.

Lily's *goal* was to have some kind of plan in place to break out of this pattern/comfort zone she has created. She also wondered if there is more to this pattern than she has realised and said that it would be good to open it up further.

Lily has tried to help herself with this issue by having a long break between relationships, asking friends and family to let her know if they think she is going down the relationship 'rabbit hole' again, but they don't want to hurt her or interfere so she is not getting the help she needs here. Finally, she started organising social events to help others but also to get to know someone before leaping into what she called the 'romantic sphere' and idealising people.

Lily listed as her strengths, outside of romantic contexts, having a good sense of people and who she can trust.

The Session

Windy: So, what's your understanding of the purpose of our conversation this afternoon, Lily?

Lily: So, I understand that you're currently writing a book about single-session therapy, a new book. Is that right?

Windy: Yeah.

Lily: And possibly looking for case studies.

Windy: Yeah, particularly on people who are stuck with a particular issue.

Lily: Yeah, on a specific issue, yeah, rather than just general.

Windy: And, so I understand from your pre-session form that you are stuck in a particular relationship pattern.

Lily: Yes. I tend to have a problem with…, I keep finding myself in relationships where I think,

'Oh wow, they're so interesting and really cool, really like them,' and it gets very serious very quickly.

Windy: What do you mean by very serious very quickly?

Lily: Well, you know ... I've had it before – this was when I was like 21, I'm 28 now, but there was one person we said, 'I love you,' after a week. We were living together at the time already, and that happened a couple of times, getting together with people I was living with as a housemate. Or my last relationship that ended about a year ago, I think... we just leapt in so quickly. I met his family after a month. I think that's pretty quick. It was like the third or fourth date. I think that's too quick.

Windy: And what would be a better timetable for you?

     [*Here, I am asking Lily to consider a time-based goal – to do something different, to break the pattern.*]

Lily: ... [*Pause*] You see, this is a question I have. I don't know if it's about constructing a timetable. Maybe something like that would be good just to say, 'OK, at least wait this amount of time,' or whether I just dig my heels in a little bit and just slow down and say, 'OK, I don't really know him yet.'

Windy: Or both.

Lily: Or both, yeah.

Windy: 'Cos it sounds like you're getting something from this pattern.

[*Rather than remain with the question of a goal, I shift to asking her what the payoff is from the pattern. It would have been better if I continued to be goal-focused.*]

Lily: … Yes.

Windy: At least part of you is anyway.

Lily: Yeah. I think it's something about… believing that, if I can help them, then they're less likely to reject me or lose interest because they depend on me. I think it's a little bit of a co-dependent structure I'm going for. And for me, on some level, that represents a kind of security.

[*To my mind, co-dependency is where one person needs another person to need them. This fits Lily quite well.*]

Windy: Security in what sense?

Lily: Security that, OK, if I know they need me, then maybe I don't need to worry as much… [*long pause*] if they're going to lose interest. I do have that anxiety a lot, like, 'Is he losing interest in me?'

Windy: What does losing interest in you mean for you?

Lily: What does it mean to me?

Windy: Yeah.

Lily: … [*Long pause*] What does it mean to me? … 'Oh, she's … not special', or something,' I don't need her.'

Windy: That's in the mind of the other person. What about for you?

Lily: Yeah.… [*Long pause*] Sure, what could that mean to me? You mean like what does it mean for me in my life, the consequences?

Windy: Well, we could say what does it mean about you, in your mind.

Lily: What does it mean about me? … [*Pause*]

Windy: If somebody is losing interest in you and doesn't think you're special, what does it mean about you in your mind?

Lily: … [*Long pause*] Something about my value, I think. Something that I … [*pause*] can give and give all I want, all I can and still not be enough, still not have value.

Windy: Have value for whom?

Lily: … [*Long pause*] Well, I think it's … [*pause*] for other people. I wanted to say 'men', but I wasn't sure about it because I often think… I stretch quite far in other relationships too and friendships; I tend to give a lot more and then think, 'Hang on, I'm giving a lot here.'

Windy: I think we have to distinguish between what other people may think is your value and what you think is your value and what's the relationship between the two, because it sounds like, and you correct me if I'm wrong, that your value to you is based on your value to other people.

                   [*I have begun to explore the dynamics of this issue with Lily. Rereading this, I am disappointed that I did not agree a session goal with Lily. I did know, from her pre-session form that she was looking to develop a plan to break out of the relationship pattern that she is discussing. I wish I had referred to this as a basis for agreeing the goal.*]

Lily: Yeah. It's strange.

Windy: And the idea is that you've figured out somehow that, if you can help people, then somehow your value to them goes up and, therefore, your value to you correspondently goes up.

Lily: ... Yeah. It's a really strange thing because I ... get confused with my confidence, my self-esteem sometimes, because I think I have quite a solid core in that sense. I think I have a really good sense of ... I really love being me. I really value myself and my life and I really like myself. And then I get into a romantic relationship and it's like something, I just have so little confidence as who I am in a relationship.

Windy: That's what I think, in terms of what you wrote in the form and I think what you're saying now, and this is not an uncommon thing when you take yourself out of a romantic arena, so to speak, and you're just doing your own thing on your own and things like that, you can feel confident and have value and things like that. But, when you enter into the relationship arena, then somehow something gets activated that's not activated when you're not in that arena. I think the kind of thing is that two things get activated: one is the idea of value – 'That my value rests on how other people value me, and the best way I've found to make sure that they value me is to help them and to continue to help them.' But there's the other aspect I wanted to pick up on the form, that somehow there's this idealising the other.

[*It would have been better for me to ask Lily what she thought of my 'value' hypothesis before beginning to discuss idealisation.*]

Lily: Yeah, absolutely.

Windy: And I'm wondering how that fits in. Is it the same issue? Is it a separate issue?

Lily: That's a good question. I think it's somewhere probably intertwined. Again, the example of my last boyfriend, I thought he was amazing and I got so quickly into that place of, 'Oh my gosh, it works so well and so many shared interests', and then anything that didn't seem quite right, I would just go, 'Yeah, but that's OK. I can make that work. We can make that work.' And my family and friends were going, 'Are you sure about this, Lily? You have quite different political views', for example, things that were really, really deeply ingrained and things that one can make work. So, I convinced myself, 'Oh, well, it's OK to have different–'

Anyway, as it turned out, after we broke out I found out not a single one of my friends liked him, not a single one of my family members liked him, but I'd imagined him as this kind of person who … yeah, would just slot in and everything worked and everything was great. And I looked back and thought, 'Oh my gosh', all those conversations I thought were really great, I think I was driving a lot of them. I was giving a lot of my energy to make things fun or making suggestions as to what we did. I would book what we were doing. And I had a great time, but I think I pour so much of my own positivity and try to drive, make it amazing, which is actually quite draining; it's not a natural thing for me, driving it, and then afterwards I think, 'Oh God.'

Windy: Did he also need help?

Lily: Yeah. He was in his 30s still talking about when he was bullied as a little boy. Just talked about it all the time and almost wanted me to comfort him a lot, and crying a lot and very, very, very vulnerable person, yeah.

Windy: And yet there's a bit in the form which stood out for me, that says, 'Once somebody told me I was the emotional backbone to their life, and I think this is what I'm subconsciously seeking out.' The emotional backbone to their life.

[*Note that I am making quite a lot of references to Lily's pre-session form which was rich in insight.*]

Lily: I know. That was my first relationship that I was in when I was 16 to 18 and I was really, really in love with him and it was very mutual and lovely. But he had a lot of problems.... And, yeah, I think I just really.... I don't know if it's love, but I loved it. Basically, I think there is something a bit ego-based around this where it's like I love the feeling of being the light in someone's life or the reasons their happy.

Windy: And what does that do for your value?

Lily: Well, it makes it feel pretty solid.

Windy: Yeah, but because you base it on something. You've got to maintain that, like, 'I'm in this great relationship', so you've got to convince yourself that it's great and you've got to edit out the bits. It's almost like you've got two different things here that are linked together: 'I'm valuable if I help somebody and I'm the emotional backbone to their life' and 'I am valuable if I'm in a special relationship with a wonderful, creative person.'

Lily: … Yeah, it has a phony feeling to it.

Windy: Yeah.

Lily: And, when I'm in it, it feels so real. That's the really jarring thing is I'm not thinking, 'Oh, this will make me feel special.' I'm thinking, 'Oh wow, this guy's so cool. This guy's so interesting. I love being around him.' And I'll tell everyone, 'This time it feels right. This time it feels really right', and they go, 'OK.' And then afterwards it's so–

Windy: How do these relationships come to an end, by the way?

Lily: I have ended most relationships I've been in. The first relationship that I mentioned we both mutually broke up because we were going to uni and whatnot, kind of carried on seeing each other after that. But every other relationship I've ended.

Windy: Why?

Lily: Because it gets to a point where I realise, 'Oh God, this is really not working. I'm starting to see the façade of what I thought it was peel away.' One person I was with, a different relationship to the ones I've mentioned, this one was someone who was suicidal and convinced I was cheating on them, and it was just such a mess. And, so, yeah, it's almost like it goes shoop – it goes really high up really quickly, all the idealising, and then it comes crashing down, and at that point it's actually quite easy for me to end it. I'm like, 'Oh, I'm done. I'm actually OK. I can walk away from this', and I haven't had such a bad healing process from breakups as I did with my first boyfriend, because that was more mutual.

Windy: Yeah. So, it sounds like, in a way, that your seeking the positive value rather than avoiding the negative value. It's almost like you're saying, 'I'm great if I'm in a great relationship and I'm the emotional backbone to somebody, if they're creative and sensitive', as the additional. And, so it's almost like a drug.

Lily: It is. It absolutely is like a drug, and the downer is awful. It's awful.

Windy: Yeah, but when you come down to it, it sounds like you are able to....

Lily: Yeah, because I realise, oh God, it doesn't feel like a massive loss like, 'I'm losing them' and 'I miss them.' It's more like, 'What an idiot I am.' So that's the heartbreak a little bit, is like I can't believe I was such an idiot again and I let this happen again.' So, it's like getting drunk and doing something stupid and then waking up.

Windy: What do you do for a living?

Lily: I'm a psychotherapist.

Windy: Right. So, a female client comes in, tells you the same story, looks to you for some advice and you say, 'What's wrong with you? You're an idiot.' That's what you'd say to these people? Would you?

[*This is therapist-led rather than client led, I decide, unilaterally, to pursue the self-devaluation. This is not good SST practice.*]

Lily: No, of course not.

Windy: Would you think that and not say it?

Lily: … [*Pause*] No. I mean, it's funny, my best friend called me at two in the morning last night saying, 'Lily, I've fallen in love again', and he calls me because he knows we're best friends but also because I come into this situation myself. And I don't think he's an idiot for it, and I wouldn't think a client was.

Windy: How would you view them?

Lily: I would think that maybe it's something like an addiction. There's something they're chasing, something that they get caught up in, and that that feels so good.

Windy: So, one thing you can start doing straight away is to recognise that, when you're saying that you're an idiot, that you're equating yourself with this addiction, which you wouldn't equate with your friends and clients; you would presumably have some compassion, understanding, accepting, but recognising that they have a problem. So that's one thing that you can do for yourself: recognising the first time that you say, 'You're an idiot, you've done it again', then, 'Whoa', and start a different type of narrative towards yourself. I think that's something that you can definitely do. But, like other addictions, you've got to recognise the signs early.

[*It would be better if I had asked Lily if she thought that adopting this stance towards herself would be helpful rather than me deciding that it would be.*]

Lily: Yeah.

Windy: I don't know if you've heard of this book by John Cleese – do you know John Cleese?

Lily: Yeah.

Windy: He wrote a book with this psychiatrist called Robin Skynner and he wrote *Families and How to Survive Them* and it was well illustrated. It reminds me of you, there was this person at a party and the thought bubble was, 'What a deliciously sick person that I'm attracted to.' So, I think one of the things that maybe you can do for yourself is start listening and what's the early warning signs for you?

[Here, I am introducing the idea of an early warning system. It would be better if I had asked Lily, 'Do you think you would benefit from developing an early warning system.]

Lily: Yeah.... I'm definitely drawn to the 'Who's that quiet one over there? They look interesting.'

Windy: Yeah.

Lily: 'Kind and sensitive.'

Windy: Yeah, sensitive, alone, quiet.

Lily: Yeah.

Windy: So maybe anything that comes under 'this person obviously needs help', I would say go up and give them your business card, if you want to do something for them. So, I think that might be something that you could do to start breaking the pattern. Who would you prefer to have a relationship with? What would have longer legs for you, do you think?

[Although, I still have not asked Lily for her session goal, at least with this question, I am asking her to think about change.]

Lily: ... I've thought about this as well and it's hard 'cos ... it's hard for me to imagine being with someone where ... we're both being proactive, we're not leaning on each other. So, in my mind, when I answer that question, I'm thinking, well, it would be great to have someone who was proactive, engaged, kind of robust and sensitive and able to have meaningful conversations. I don't want someone who's macho.

Windy: No, I understand that. But it sounds like they've got the sensitivity without the obvious 'help me' vulnerability.

Lily: Yeah.

Windy: It's almost like you've got this radar for the vulnerable.

Lily: Yeah. When I'm at a party, well, it tends to happen if I'm not having such a great time at the party, whatever, and then, if someone loses something, I think, 'I'll help them find this object.' It feels so satisfying to me.

Windy: Right. So, again, that may be a mundane example, but how would you feel if you didn't help them?

Lily: ... Like it feels like a wasted opportunity to have made a connection. I don't know, how would I feel? ... I'd feel like, 'Oh God, that's really rubbish of me that I could've done and I didn't.'

Windy: Well, yes, but, if you didn't have a problem in that area, if you could help somebody and you weren't going to, don't forget this is your addiction. This is your vulnerability. So, is it rubbish if you don't accept the opportunity to practise your addiction? Is that rubbish?

Lily: … [*Long pause*]

Windy: What are you thinking of?

Lily: I was just going to say I've started organising socials and inviting guys and girls, 'cos dating apps can be really– It's another way I'm starting to switch up my pattern. If I meet someone one to one, I think that idealising is a lot easier to happen. When you have a group of people, you slow things down, you're not talking to them all the time, it's a bit more organic. So that's one way I've started to do that.

Windy: Yeah, I think that's creating good conditions. I think that's one thing. I think the other thing that occurred to me when I was reading that is what happens if you meet somebody in that setting? What I'm saying is be careful who you get drawn to.

Lily: Yes. … Yeah, and I've been drawn to some people … yeah, and wondered, 'What is this about?'

Windy: How quickly does you helping them dynamic come into the conversation?

Lily: ... [*Long pause*] It's a tricky thing. I don't know that I did so much to help the last guy I was with, for example. I don't think I was there doing so much.

Windy: No, it sounds like the other dynamic was the wonderfulising.

Lily: ... Yeah. There is a commonality in that they're all really fragile, really, really fragile and needing help. It's not that I can necessarily help. But the question was how early on.

Windy: Yeah, how quickly do you notice they're fragile?

Lily: That takes a little while. It's almost like I see all the really fun, shiny things first and then after, let's say a month or two, something like that, I start going, 'Oh.' But I'm so in it by that point that I'm not really deeply considering it.

Windy: Yeah. So, what are you saying, the wonderfulising/idealising bit comes first and then it emerges that they are fragile and then you're into it and then you help them because you're into it? Is that what you're saying?

Lily: … It feels like such a blur. I remember just thinking, 'Wow, he's amazing, really interesting, shared values in some things' and 'There's a chemistry. There's a connection.' I'm not really aware or thinking about, 'Does this guy seem robust?' or whatever. I'm just thinking, 'How do I feel?' It's all in the feeling. And then I tell my family about it and they say, 'Oh, OK, we'll see', and then I tell them, 'Oh, by the way, he said this and he thinks this about this', and they'll go, 'Are you sure about this, Lily?' and I'm going, 'La la la la, yes, it's fine.'

Windy: You block it out, then.

Lily: Yeah.

Windy: So, what could you do differently at that point?

[*This is better from me, asking about change.*]

Lily: … [*Long pause*] It's really, really hard to see what this other person is seeing, like to see what my parents are seeing, to see what my friends are seeing, because I think to myself, 'Well, they don't see what I see. They don't see the wonderful stuff, so they're probably not getting it.' So, at the time, I'm thinking they're the ones who aren't seeing. But, actually, I do think that, even if you haven't met the person, just hearing about how things are going, how quickly they're going, I think people tend to have quite a good idea.

Windy: Do you have anybody who's on your side but ruthlessly honest with you who you could almost form a dating reflection group that you can use to touch base with early on?

[*In SST, we not only encourage people to draw on their own internal resources, we encourage them to draw on their external resources.*]

Lily: … Well, I think I mentioned, so both of my parents, I think they're in this position of, 'Look, we're gonna tell you but we don't want to interfere. We're gonna let you do your thing. We're not gonna try and control.' So, yes, but they haven't got the bluntness. And then my friend, Molly, who I wrote about, she can be ruthlessly honest but she told a white lie the last time. So, I've said to her, 'Please just tell me. I can take it.' I think she's more likely than anybody. But some people are like, 'I didn't want to hurt your feelings,' 'cos if I'm saying, 'Oh my God, I'm gonna marry this guy,' and they think, 'Well, what if she does?'

Windy: You could tell them, 'It hurts my feelings when you don't hurt my feelings.'

Lily: Yeah.

Windy: The reason I say that is because in Alcoholics Anonymous everyone has a buddy or a mentor that they can connect with.

Lily: Yeah. ... So true. It does hurt my feelings when they think I can't take hurt feelings. Of course I can take hurt feelings...

Windy: Where do you live?

Lily: I live in Central London with my parents.

Windy: It's interesting, there used to be a group in Central London, I don't know if it's still going, it's called the Sex and Love Addiction Group or SLAG. It sounds like it's difficult for you to give yourself that level of objectivity. And I'm just thinking, OK, you might need some people on your team. And, if Molly can be on your team, fine. If you go to one of these Sex and Love Addiction Groups, they'll give you the feedback.

Lily: Interesting.

Windy: It's something for you to explore and consider. How do you feel about that suggestion?

Lily: Yeah, it's interesting. I have thought about love addiction.... What I guess I don't associate with is I don't feel like I'm possessive. There's a shade of that addiction that can be possessiveness, jealousy, clinginess.

Windy: No, you're not that. I mean, what are the features? You get swept up very quickly. You lose a sense of objectivity. You put your rose-coloured glasses on. You can't see what other people see and you don't want to see what other people see. Just because you're not jealous and possessive, it doesn't mean you're not addicted. Look, the word addiction is fraught, but I think just listening to you, I think there are things that you can do for yourself, and that is to develop a list of warning signs. I think that's important. I've got my bag of tricks here. Dryden is waving his red flag. I would definitely say that's what you can do for yourself. Based on a thorough review of your past relationships, what can you write down are the red flags that you need to learn from?

[By waving a physical red flag, I want Lily to remember what her task is in bringing about change to this pattern. Although, I suggested that she seek help from external resources, basically her task is to develop a list of warning signs or red flags that 'feel' positive at the time but only serve to maintain the very cycle that Lily wants to break.]

Lily: … [*Pause*] Yes.

Windy: Of course, the idea is are you prepared to give up the high?

Lily: Yeah…. [*Long pause*] Yeah, and I suppose it's tricky because I think it's not the only element but there is the added element of someone putting on their best face as well. I'm not just working with my illusion; it's them. We're both giving each other impressions to begin with and putting on a face. You know what I mean?

Windy: Yeah. When you meet somebody and you have a sense that this could be 'the one', how often do you see them?

Lily: … [*Pause*] Once a week or twice in a week max.

Windy: And texting and phoning?

Lily: Yeah, a lot of texting.

Windy: Right, so that's something that you can maybe get a hold of, 'cos once a week is fine, meeting them, but I think the texting and things like that, how would you feel about slowing that down?

[Here, I suggest that Lily consider decreasing the amount of texting she does in order to reduce the intensity of her 'high'.]

Lily: That would be great because I think that raises my anxiety, and it makes it a lot easier for me to form a picture of what someone is through their texts. I think, 'Oh, that.' I'm very good at imagining something based off very little information.

Windy: Yes, and that's something that, again, would be a red flag and you might say, 'Well, OK, what I'm going to do is I'm going to limit myself to texts,' and that will slow things down. What other things do you do that reinforce the pattern?

Lily: … *[Long pause]* Like I said, I think I put a lot of effort into… book a date or I'm the one who's deciding and cooking dinner.

Windy: Maybe you could introduce the 50/50 rule.

[Another suggestion to break the pattern.]

Lily: Yeah.

Windy: 'Cos it sounds like you're driving the bus.

Lily: Yeah.

Windy: In my day this was the man's job, you realise that. But maybe that's another thing that you might want to do, to recognise that it's not equal.

Lily: There is something interesting, I'm also quite drawn to effeminate qualities. If you look at it from another perspective, I'm taking the position of a more alpha – alpha's too strong, but a sort of taking charge and looking after and protecting and, 'I'll look after you,' kind of thing. And then this person, I think they also become more, in response to me coming forward so much, they go limp and don't dispute. They think, 'Oh, she'll do it.'

Windy: Yeah, and then they become dependent upon you doing it. That's the danger. So those are the signs, and I think that, if you can almost keep a diary about who does what: 'OK, I've booked a table this time,' or see if they suggest booking a table. If they suggest and say, 'Can you book a table?' and you say, 'No, you book a table. I did it last time.' How's that landing?

Lily: Yeah, I think it sounds good. I've got to do something because I'd love to have a relationship that felt balanced. But it feels very foreign to me.

Windy: Well, change is strange.

Lily: … Yeah.

Windy: So, any childhood roots of this behaviour, do you think? Anything that you can think of?

[It would have been better if I had instead suggested to Lily that she formalise a list of red flags and counters to these flags. We had begun to do this, but in a rather unsystematic way.]

Lily: I don't know. I think there might be a thing with my mum and dad, but they're very helpful with each other. It's not like one of them's pathetic and the other one's taking over. But I think there's anxiety in both of them and a lot of their dynamic is… *[pause]* I guess looking after each other. I think they have a good, solid thing that I haven't quite – I mean, I was in therapy for years and I couldn't find a specific thing, although I had, for some reason, and this is very odd, that, when my grandmother died when I was six I was devastated. I really, really loved my grandmother. And I remember at age six I'd for some reason got it into my head I could've saved her. It was my fault. I could've saved her. And I believed it so strongly and I felt so ashamed that I didn't tell anyone that I believed that, and I held that feeling. It was really crushing. It had nothing to do with me, but for some reason I thought this is my fault. I don't know if that's a religious sentiment that I'd gotten from being a religious child, but something about saving and all that. But I don't know.

I had it as well when I worked in psychiatric hospitals. There was a patient who I became really attached to, really, really cared for them a lot, and then they left the hospital and I was convinced, I thought, 'Oh my God, I could've saved him. Something awful's going to happen to that guy and I could've saved him.' It's bizarre.

Windy: So you've got this idea of the saviour.

[*This brief look at the past has led to another aspect of the issue, 'Lily as saviour'.*]

Lily: Yeah.

Windy: And, when you do think you're saving people, it sounds like that gives you a good feeling.

Lily: Yeah.

Windy: And, if you bypass an opportunity – this is why I'm saying, if you get involved with somebody who's fragile and you don't help them, like going back to that party and somebody's lost something and you're saying, 'Well, I ain't gonna help.' I think you're gonna find that difficult, it sounds like. So, you may need to rethink that, the idea that, 'OK, that's my first thought, but let me stand back and think about this.' Do you have that power?

Lily: To stand back and think about it?

Windy: No, to save people.

Lily: Right, do I have that power? ... No.

Windy: Would you like that power?

Lily: Honestly, yeah, thinking about it, it's like ... yeah, I don't think I would really want to do that.

Windy: No, and incidentally it's difficult to have a relationship with a God. But that's how six-year-olds think, isn't it? That, 'Somehow, I could've saved my grandmother.' But, if you think it through, it's really like a saviour idea and that you get a good feeling when you're saving people and also a good feeling when you're in this wonderful. I think there are two different related dynamics going on which I think you need to pay attention to.

Lily: Two different things.

Windy: Yeah, it's related. They're both saying, 'This is the way I get value: saving people and being with wonderful people. And I'm waving my red flag furiously.'

Lily: The addiction part, though, is obsession. I'd say the main symptom of this is obsession, complete obsession as well. I cannot stop thinking about them. Everything I see is almost them tinted.

Windy: Yes. I mean, addiction is not exactly the right word, but I think the obsessionality and, of course, the more you feed that, the more it will grow. So, at the early signs when you start thinking about that, you say, 'OK, I'm gonna give this five minutes' thought and then I'm gonna go onto something else. And, if I find that difficult, I'm going to really get involved in something else.' Do you have any hobbies and things you're really interested in, in life, apart from saving wonderful men?

Lily: Well, I haven't dated anyone since that guy. We broke up at the end of 2023, so then I've been single, not been on many dates at all. I think I went on two dates with this one guy. Didn't work out.

Windy: I'm asking do you get involved in things that are not related to dating?

Lily: Yeah, but just to give you context, I don't do that much. So outside of it I love to travel. So, I spend months in different places. I work remotely, so I get to do that. I love that sense of adventure, doing things that are a bit frightening when I'm going travelling – rafting and various things. That was really fun and not something I'd normally do. I love … art … movies.

Windy: Appreciating or creating?

Lily: Both, but art is something I've not created in a long time.

Windy: You may want to think about doing that, because what I'm trying to think is obsessionality loves a vacuum; if you haven't got anything else going on in your life – OK, travelling's important to you, but you're not going to be travelling a lot, so obsessionality loves, 'Oh, this person's not doing anything. Come on, Lads, let's pile in.' So, I think that might be useful. When you start to date, I think there's a lot of things that you need to watch out for because I think you mindlessly get into things. Not mindlessly, but very easily without thinking. That's why I'm suggesting some sort of external touch base with people.

[*Again, I wished I had suggested that Lily formalise the process of (a) responding to red flags – including saviour and idealising thoughts and behaviour and (b) beginning to do constructive things that will break the pattern when she starts dating again.*]

Lily: Yeah. Organising socials is a new thing that I think I've put a lot of energy into and I love. I love it because I bring people together, strangers, a mix of strangers and friends, and 20 of us will go out to a bar or 10 of us will go and see some music. That's something I can really pour a lot of that obsessional energy into. I think I have hoards of it.

Windy: Maybe the rule might be that you don't date somebody in your circle, so that you don't get caught up in that. That really it's just separate from that. You might want to think that one through a little bit.

Lily: Really? Because part of the reason I'm doing that is to slow it down so that I might meet someone in that context and it's actually quite nice because we've met.

Windy: Yeah, I get that as well. I'm just saying you may want to think about that as you go forward.

Lily: OK.

Windy: Listen, our time is coming to an end. I'm just wondering what you're gonna take away from this that might help you to get unstuck from this particular pattern?

Lily: I think a lot of what we've talked about has been really, really helpful. 'Change is strange' is definitely a big one. If it feels familiar and I'm getting hooked and that feeling is coming back, it's like maybe there's something about this feeling and I can step back from it a little bit and, if I can help it, not get swept up so much. And, also something about pouring my obsessional energy into more things. I feel like I already have lots of things I spend time doing and I love my work, but, yeah, if there's a guy, it just takes over. So, finding a way to dampen that, tone it down a bit with other things. Yeah, developing warning signs. Yeah. I've still got this question of what is it that I'm seeking? What is this thing about I'm not valuable unless I'm helpful? But I don't know.

Windy: I don't think it is. I think it's, 'I am valuable if I'm helpful.' I think you're seeking a high value. I don't think this is necessarily a low self-esteem thing. It's almost like, 'I'm addicted to high self-esteem,' and the positivity that goes about creating this wonderful relationship and, 'I'm helping, so I'm really doing good here.'

Lily: OK, that makes sense, because I am thinking where is the void? I'm sure we all have voids and insecurities, but that does make sense that it's more about the high.

Windy: So, I'll send you a recording of this and then later the transcript. In a couple of months I'll send you an evaluation form and you can let me know what you made of it, both on the day and then afterwards.

Lily: OK, great. Thank you so much, Windy.

Lily's Follow-up Questionnaire

Date: 01/4/25

Question	Response
1. What progress did you make on the issue that you brought to the session. Indicate the amount of progress you have made on this issue by using a 0% (no progress) – 100% (problem solved) scale.	**Issue Brought to the Session (Please name this):** A strong pattern in my romantic relationships where I leap into serious relationships with people who are very fragile or unavailable, lacking in emotional maturity and resilience. **Amount of progress made:** 60% I have been attracted to some people I've met, and the excitement did grow to an intense level at times, but even when it reached a peak, the attraction did fade as I got to know them. This has never really happened before and allows me to see how fleeting and not real this feeling can be, and how important it is to get to know someone better with time. I feel I had much more patience and self awareness when the red flags started waving…

	Factors that helped me make progress: With Windy's advice, I have slowed down a lot in terms of getting to know people first before leaping in. I have realised the importance of being friends with someone rather than jump straight into a relationship before we know each other well. **Factors that were absent that could have helped me make more progress:** Due to frequent travel, testing / making progress has been a little challenging in the longer term.
2. Did you make any progress on other issues that you have that you did not bring to our session? Please elaborate.	N/A
3. How would you describe your relationship with Windy Dryden in the session?	I believe Windy and I formed a connection relatively quickly during our session. I sensed a warm and trusting dynamic between us, and I felt genuinely heard and understood.

4. What, if anything, did Windy Dryden do during the session that was helpful to you?	I found Windy's humour uplifting and helped removed a great deal of judgement and anger towards myself that I have been carrying since my last breakup. He encouraged me to have some self-compassion in the same way I would towards a friend. I have noticed a lot of change in this area. I found him waving the red flag hilarious. I also found his comment that he doesn't think this is coming from a deep insecurity really interesting and one I hadn't considered before. I always had assumed it must be something buried deep down, which it may be, but I agree that it's more to do with an intense attraction to the 'high' and euphoria of love.
5. What, if anything, did Windy Dryden do during the session that was unhelpful to you?	I didn't find anything unhelpful.
6. How helpful did you find the pre-session form if you were sent one? Please elaborate.	I found the form helpful. It was quite affronting to write down issues in this way and I did feel vulnerable sending it off – it felt like a real commitment to discuss the problem head-on, one which I felt ashamed about, so no turning back! But I liked that a lot as it felt it required courage and commitment from me.

7. How helpful did you find the audio-recording of your session? Please elaborate.	I didn't listen to the audio recording, I would prefer not to!
8. How helpful did you find the transcript of your sessions? Please elaborate.	I had a read of the transcript and didn't find it helpful or unhelpful.
9. How does Single-Session Therapy compare with other therapies that you have had? Please elaborate.	I found it entertaining and uplifting, which actually was incredibly helpful because it brought levity to my situation. I loved the reference to the John Cleese cartoon, 'deliciously sick'... this really stayed with me because I no longer felt so alone with the issue. I really love the playfulness of having props, how concise the experience is, how Windy was really skilled at interrupting as needed and keeping to the most important points. I also very much liked his questions, I found them helpfully challenging.

10. What improvements, if any, do you think need to be made to the Single-Session Therapy framework?	I wouldn't make any improvements.
11. Please give any additional feedback that your responses to the questions above have not covered.	N/A

My Reflections and Summary

On her pre-session form, Lily stated that she wanted to discuss a strong pattern in her romantic relationships where she leaps into serious relationships with people who are very fragile or unavailable, lacking in emotional maturity and resilience. Her goal was to find some kind of plan to break this pattern. She said that with my advice, she has slowed down a lot in terms of getting to know people first before leaping in. She realised the importance of being friends with someone rather than jumping straight into a relationship before she knows the other person well. However, due to travel commitments she has not had an opportunity to implement her takeaways.

I thought that my work with Lily was good in parts. We were able to focus on her relationship pattern throughout the session and did discuss some helpful pattern-breaking factors that could contribute to the development of an overall plan. However, I could have been more systematic in the way I did this. I was not as goal focused as I needed to be in the session. If I had been we would both have been clearer at what we were aiming to achieve in our conversation.

In terms of our therapeutic relationship, Lily said that she believed that we formed a connection relatively quickly during the session. She sensed a warm and trusting dynamic between us, and she felt genuinely heard and understood. Concerning what I did that was helpful in the session, Lily said she found my humour uplifting and helped removed a great deal of judgement and anger towards herself that she had been carrying since her last breakup. She said that I encouraged her to have some self-compassion in the same way she would towards a friend. Lily noticed a lot of change in this area. Lily said that she found my waving the red flag hilarious. She also said that she found my comment that he doesn't think this pattern is coming from a deep insecurity really interesting and one she hadn't considered before. She always assumed it must be something buried deep down, which it still may be, but she agreed that it's more to do with an intense attraction to the 'high' and euphoria of love.

Regarding the pre-session form, recording, and transcript, Lily mentioned the following. She found the pre-session found the form helpful. She said that it was challenging to write down issues in this way and she did feel vulnerable sending it off. However, she also said that it felt like a real commitment to discuss the problem head-on, one which she felt ashamed about, so there was no turning back! But she said she liked that a lot as it felt it required courage and commitment from her. Lily did not listen to the audio and while she read the transcript she found it neither helpful nor helpful.

8

Dealing with Stuckness in Making a Full Career Change

Date: 28-01-25
Time: 36 mins 10 secs

Lottie's Pre-Session Form

Lottie said that she wanted to discuss the stuckness she experiences that is preventing her from fully changing her career. Her goal from the session was to see a path towards a more fulfilling career that is alignment with what she referred as her 'soul's purpose'. She said that thus path might include being helped to identify resources and looking at what practical steps could be taken, The steps that she has taken to deal with this issue e.g., writing an entry for a counselling directory and designing a website have not lead to her taking action, which is unlike her. She I usually good at taking action in other areas of her life.

In addition to being good at taking action and getting things done, Lottie listed her strengths as being organised, resilient and approachable.

The Session

Windy: So, Lottie, what's your understanding of the purpose of our conversation this afternoon?

Lottie: My understanding is that you're looking for people who have got an issue where they're stuck and that you will employ the single-session therapy method and it'll be used potentially in a book that you are writing, potentially, and it'll be anonymised.

Windy: And you have an issue that falls under that heading that you would like to address with me?

Lottie: Yes. Did you get my form?

Windy: Yes, I did.

Lottie: So, you've got the form.

Windy: I've got the form, yeah. So why don't you, very briefly, put it into your own words what you're stuck with at the moment?

Lottie: OK. So, what I'm stuck with is I qualified as a therapist in 2019, just before Covid, and I was potentially looking over the next couple of years from there, so by about 2021 I was looking to become almost like a full-time therapist and give up the day job.

Windy: When you say 'almost like a full-time therapist'.

Lottie: Well, maybe be a full-time therapist and then have something else on the side that isn't what I'm doing as a day job now. So maybe something related. I don't know, working in a therapy centre where you're not actually seeing clients. So, I was hoping to transition over to this new way of life and move as well. But, obviously Covid happened and then my dad passed away in 2021 as well. And it feels like I've got really stuck. So, I've got a small practice that I see clients in the evenings within the UKCP minimum. I think it's four clients they ask you to see a week so that you keep your accreditation. And I'm moving, hopefully, next month.

So, it's a nice time now to think about that geographical element and positioning myself somewhere where I can make connections with people. But I feel really stuck in terms of getting even the basic, like writing a counselling directory profile, putting together a webpage. I can't seem to do it and it's very unlike me, because I work in journalism and communications. So, I write webpage content all the time, but I just can't seem to do it for me.

Windy: Let me just ask you – we could change this if we need to in the transcript, but where are you moving from and to?

Lottie: I'm moving from Brentwood. Do you know where Brentwood is?

Windy: Yes, in Essex.

Lottie: And I'm moving to St Leonard's-on-Sea in East Sussex. So not too far, but a different way of life, I feel.

Windy: Yes, indeed. So, you have the writing skills. It's not as if you don't have the writing skills.

Lottie: Yeah. That's what's frustrating.

Windy: But you find yourself stopping yourself.

Lottie: Yeah. I write like a few sentences or I might have a look at what someone else has written and try and get some inspiration. But it's like a block comes down and I think, 'Oh no, I don't know what to write. I don't feel like I can put the words together.'

    [*It would have been better if I had asked Lottie for her session goal. She had mentioned this on the form, but it is better for this to made explicit by the person at the outset of the session.*]

Windy: Let's suppose somebody called Lottie was to engage you as a journalist and gave you all the information about her that's you, and she engaged you to write an engaging profile, would you be able to do it?

Lottie: … [*Pause*] Yeah.

Windy: If it wasn't for you.

Lottie: Yeah, it would feel easier if I was writing it almost about somebody else, like I'm taking myself out of it and looking in. Yeah, it would be easier.

Windy: Yeah. And you'd be able to do that, would you?

Lottie: Yes.

Windy: What was that looking up?

Lottie: Yes, I would. Because, when I say something, I like to be definite. Yes, I would.

Windy: OK. So, what's the difference? Since the information is the same and you writing it would be the same, so what's the difference between the two scenarios?

[*I ask this question to discover the block.*]

Lottie: I think, 'cos you're taking yourself out. … It's like a part of you would be writing it so you could almost get into that part and get the job done, but, when it's me and all my other parts and all the different anxieties.

Windy: OK, but presumably there's more to Lottie than just a therapist. You don't come alive to see those four clients and then it's like Dracula – you take the blood out of the four clients and then you go back into your grave.

Lottie: I don't, yeah.

Windy: There's more to you than that. But there's something. What do you call it? Is it a fear-type block?

Lottie: It's a fear of judgement amongst probably my peers and perhaps people who are higher above me as well, like people who are lecturers at the college I was at. I feel like people will be judging what I write. That's one of the fears.

Windy: You mean you're scared that they're gonna say, 'This is a beautifully written piece about a potentially emerging therapist'?

[I am fully aware that this is not Lottie's fear, but I want her to be clear that she has a fear of negative judgement, not a fear of judgement.]

Lottie: No, I think they'd say, 'Look at what she's writing. Huh!' Yeah, it would be negative. I don't know why, though.

Windy: And would you agree with that?

Lottie: No.

Windy: So, you're basically scared of a judgement that you don't agree with.

Lottie: Yeah. … [*Pause*] Well, part of me doesn't agree and then there's another part that's like back in 2019 when I left. So, it's like I'm stuck.

Windy: Well, back in 2019, OK, there's the part of you back in 2019. What's that part of you?

[*Working with different parts of a person is common in SST.*]

Lottie: So, when I was trying to find a supervisor, I struggled with that just because nobody seemed to have any space, and I took it personally, but it might just be that they didn't have space.

Windy: 'Is that Lottie? Alright, 'We're full.' If Lottie contacts you, we're full!'

Lottie: 'She's awful!' And I felt like there were a lot of doors closing. It was interesting. And then

because Covid happened, I didn't really get
going. I couldn't get out there to prove. I felt
like I was stifled a little bit. But I must admit,
I'd say in the last year, actually, I've gained
a little bit more confidence, but it's still
quite…

Windy: When you say you've gained a little bit of
confidence, what do you mean?

[*This is a typical SST response. The person
mentions a change for the better and I want
to understand and help the person develop
it.*]

Lottie: By keeping clients and working with issues
by doing some CPD, working with issues in
a different way than maybe I would've done
when I was on my course. So, I've learnt.

Windy: So, what 'self' do you think you'd have to
have for this not to be a block for you? What
attitude do you think you'd have to have
towards yourself that would then lead you to
engage with the task of writing profiles?

Lottie: And trying to get more clients.

Windy: Yeah, what view of yourself would you have
to have?

Lottie: … [*Long pause*] That I'm competent and
capable and a safe pair of hands.… [*Pause*]

Yeah…. It's the idea of having a picture. As I'm thinking about it, I've got this idea of a photo and these words.

Windy: Competent, what else was it?

Lottie: Competent, a safe pair of hands.

Windy: There were three things.

Lottie: Yeah, I can't remember the first thing. Competent, maybe capable.

Windy: Capable, yeah. Competent, capable and a safe pair of hands.

Lottie: Yeah. And I think that maybe if I'd done some other courses, maybe I'd feel more confident, if I was doing more CPD. It all kind of comes together, in a way. So, I was thinking about maybe doing EDMR.

Windy: Not a good idea (waving finger). So, you mean you've got to have the feeling of competency, confidence and being a safe pair of hands first before.

[*Quite often people believe that they need a set of conditions – like being competent, capable and a safe pair of hands – to be in place before doing something. I want to see if this is the case with Lottie.*]

Lottie: You put yourself out there. That's what it is, putting yourself out there.

Windy: Do you think everybody does that? Nobody puts themselves out there until they're confident, capable or a safe pair of hands?

Lottie: … [*Pause*] I think there's a lot of bullshitters and egos and people who believe themselves. They've got this sense of confidence that I don't, particularly if I've seen something they've written and I've thought, 'Oh, I don't agree with what they've said.' So, I'm judging as well.

Windy: But what are you judging?

Lottie: What they've written and that I don't agree with it.

Windy: Yeah, but are you judging them or what they've written?

Lottie: Both, I guess. I'm thinking they're a bullshitter, yeah.

Windy: On the basis of bullshit.

Lottie: Yeah. They've written a load of nonsense.

Windy: I think that might be part of the problem. It sounds like you equate a part of a person with the whole person. If somebody write bullshit, they're a bullshitter.

[I don't like this intervention. My intention is to distinguish between a part of a person and the whole of a person, but I neither explain what my intention is nor do I ask Lottie if she is interested in my 'take'. Perhaps unsurprisingly, she does not show much interest in this point.]

Lottie: Yeah. I think what it is, I've seen them in action and I think they've got a high sense of self-importance. Do you know when somebody's very, and I'm thinking, 'Wow!' and they're charging £130 a session, and you're thinking, 'That's a lot.' I don't know. I suppose I just don't have that. I feel like I'm quite authentic and I don't want to be a bullshitter. I'd rather just write something from the heart.

Windy: OK. So, part of your authenticity, if we take that as a base, what would you write about yourself?

[Here, I begin to help her construct a profile from a position of authenticity. However, I am neither explicit about doing so, nor do I determine whether she will find this helpful.]

Lottie: … *[Pause]* I can't quite get the words. This is really difficult now. Something around the safety aspect, something around listening and not judging, something around coming from the heart space. I don't quite know how I'd put that in words. Something that's genuine. I might put a little bit about my work history, maybe a few lines but nothing too detailed, and say what I gained from that that I could bring to a therapeutic relationship. Yeah.

Windy: So, it would be authentic, it would be that working with you would be safe, that you would be somebody that would be compassionate – is that from the heart?

Lottie: Yeah, compassionate.

Windy: In terms of confidence and capability, where does confidence and capability come from?

Lottie: Experience.

Windy: Right. How much experience have you got?

Lottie: … 2015 is when I started my course.

Windy: Right.

Lottie: And doing placements with clients, yeah. So we're coming up to 10 years, aren't we? Blimey.

Windy: We are. We're coming up to 10 years.

Lottie: I've just realised that, yeah. Wow!

[Taking this tack is helping Lottie to see that she has some of the qualities that she has questioned.]

Windy: So, you can put that in: 'I've been in the profession for 10 years.' Do you think you have to mention confidence and competence?

Lottie: No. I think it can just come across in the way you address yourself.

Windy: Would you be happy with that: 'I'm a person who you can trust, as being a safe counsellor who's compassionate,' and all the rest of it? Is that something that you can live with?

Lottie: Yes. I can live with that. And now I'm thinking what I could say. It's starting to flow a little bit more now. I'm thinking about I could say how I like working. So, I like working creatively, so with maybe sand trays or visualisations, drawings. So that kind of work is appealing.

Windy: Right. And, if you brought your journalistic self to those bare bones, do you think you'd be able to create something that would be to your satisfaction?

[Here, I am drawing on Lottie's experience as a journalist to help her see that she can develop what we have started into a profile.]

Lottie: ... Yeah. I think I would. And now I'm thinking I could create a skeleton and create a basic profile and then maybe I'd want to add to it in the future. I'd want to add that kind of caveat that I'd want to develop.

Windy: Sure, but you can go live now.

Lottie: Yeah. Now I'm thinking of a photo, because you have to have a photo, don't you?

Windy: Yeah. Well, it depends upon what kind of photo you want. You want a glam photo? 'Cos some people look as if they've been photoshopped.

Lottie: Airbrushed. I know, I've seen a few.

Windy: Or do you want to have somebody who you trust to take some photos and you choose one?

Lottie: Yeah. I think that's what I need to do.

Windy: Now, if you did that, what would be stopping you from doing that?

[Having developed a practical plan, I am asking to see if there any obstacles.]

Lottie: … [*Pause*] At the moment, just in the next few weeks it would be the practicalities around time, because I'm hoping to move. I'm literally waiting to hear on an exchange date.

Windy: How long would it take for you to do that?

Lottie: If I wrote it?

Windy: Yeah.

Lottie: … I'd want to come back to it a few times, I wouldn't just want to bash it out and then say, 'Right, yeah, that's done.' I'd want to revisit a few times. So probably … a few days, not completely 24 hours.

Windy: How many hours then do you think it'll take you to write that?

Lottie: …   Under 10. Around 10, I'd say. I'd want to do a bit of research as well.

Windy: OK. So, when are you moving?

Lottie: I don't know yet. That's the thing. It's all a bit up in the air. Possibly mid-February.

Windy: OK. So, let's say 14th. You've got 16 days. Can you find 10 hours in 16 days?

Lottie: ... Yeah.... Yes. I'm just thinking like a Sunday, a few hours and then maybe sneak a few hours when I'm meant to be working on it. Yeah.

Windy: Do you have a family?

Lottie: No. Well, I do have an elderly mum that needs a bit of attention, but I can fit it in around her.

Windy: Yeah, when she's asleep.

Lottie: She lives somewhere else.

Windy: So that's getting over the practical elements of the block. What about the psychological aspects of the block? What about if people read that and they say, 'Really?'

[Having established with Lottie that she can implement the plan from a practical perspective, I am now enquiring about the psychological aspects of the block.]

Lottie: 'What's she going on about?'

Windy: 'What's she going on about?' right. Can you allow people to think that about you and be wrong about you?

[*My point here is that people have the right to think anything they want about and they can be right or wrong.*]

Lottie: Yeah. There's a feisty part that's coming out now that's like, 'Yeah, I bloody well can.'

[*It is great when a person spontaneously comes up with a strength that can be used going forward.*]

Windy: That's the bit that you want to bring to the table: the feisty Lottie.

Lottie: … Yeah.

Windy: There was a 'but' there you were coming out with.

Lottie: I was thinking, yeah, I've got to make sure that the judgemental – it almost feels a bit timid, that part comes in and it's like, 'What about this, though?' … But I'm OK with that.

Windy: What about what?

Lottie: 'What about this? What are they gonna say? And they'll be able to see how much you charge…. Look at that photo of you, you look awful.'

Windy: Well, OK, fine. Do you believe that people have the freedom of thought?

Lottie: Yes. It's just not very nice, is it? But I won't know about it.

Windy: You won't know about it, unless we form the Lottie Facebook Group which is all about making fun of Lottie.

Lottie: Of her. Profiles, yeah. ... And I quite like the idea of putting a geographical location on it. That has been very important to me. So, putting Y – I want to put that on there. So that's a motivating factor, as well, actually. I don't know why it's so important for me to be geographically solid. I've no idea where that came from.

Windy: I was thinking, the feisty bit we could bring the warrior part of you. Do you know why I say that?

Lottie: No.

Windy: St Leonard's Warrior Square.

Lottie: Do you know the area?

Windy: I have a flat in Eastbourne, so not too far away. I hear St Leonard's Warrior Square a lot. You could bring the feisty warrior from St Leonard's to the table.

Lottie: I like that.

[*I am very much against manualising SST. Rather, it is a mode of therapy delivery needs to be practised creatively. This is one such creative response.*]

Windy: So, if you recognise that you can actually allow people to think what they think, and actually you don't know what they're gonna be thinking.

Lottie: No, that's true.

Windy: In fact, some people would say that you're projecting into their minds what's in your mind.

Lottie: I know. I was thinking that myself.

Windy: Yeah. So, we have met the enemy and it is us. Maybe you could say, 'Well, OK, is there a part of me that's judging me and maybe I need to have a look at that part of me.'

[*Here, I am suggesting that Lottie consider the possibility of projection.*]

Lottie: That judgy part, yeah. That hasn't developed since 2019, but there's another part that has.

Windy: Yeah, that's right.

Lottie: Gosh, it's tricky. Then I've got to get onto a website, but that's after the profile. I think the profile thing I'll do first.

Windy: The profile first, yeah, and then the website. What's the job you're doing at the moment?

Lottie: I do work in communications, which is a bit like marketing but it's more working with stakeholders, like newsletters, websites, press releases.

Windy: What do you do there, then?

Lottie: So I have to put together like an information pack to inform communities about work that's going on in their area at the moment.

Windy: So, if you get that part of you that is really accepting of you, that you're a therapist who may be doing a good job with some people and not so much with others, like the rest of us, that confidence comes from doing things unconfidently and moving forward like that, and that the judgement is about you, really, and what you think about you and you're projecting it into others, unless you fear specific people judging you. Do you fear specific people who you know are judgemental?

[*Here, I was intending to pick up on the information pack idea and outline information elements that Lottie could have in her own pack, but I waylaid myself with considering the possibility that Lotties feared specific judgemental people. It would have better to have kept these separate.*]

Lottie: No. Well, there's a lot of people from my course, but that's not particular individuals. It's generally. I'm not so worried about a general therapeutic community, people who went to other institutions. They feel a bit further away. But it's just these particular. I don't know why. It's really interesting 'cos you feel like you've moved on from six years ago.

Windy: When you look at these people, when you know these people, I'm trying to figure out with you whether it's you that's judging or it would really be them that's judging you?

Lottie: ... [*Pause*] I think some people there would be judging me.

Windy: Yeah, and do they judge each other?

Lottie: Yes, they've got that kind of judginess. I don't even think that's a word.

Windy: Does it stop them from actually putting themselves forward?

Lottie: No, they've put themselves forward 'cos they've got this bullshitter armour on, whereas I don't have the armour. So, it's things like, you know when you do groupwork on a course and people who you've clashed with that you still haven't quite resolved things with, that type of thing. And then there's other people that are projecting, I don't know, different jealousy, envy. I feel like they would see me pop up.

Windy: And, of course, everybody has to love you before you can go forward.

Lottie: Yeah. Actually, I don't mind people disliking me in some areas. It's just for this it feels quite personal and quite delicate. Like I want to get it right.

Windy: Well, that's right. You can get it right, but, if you get it wrong, as you said earlier, you can put it right later. Even websites, they're not written in stone.

Lottie: No.

Windy: You can actually change things. A lot of people tweak their websites and things like that. But I think that this personal bit, it sounds like, yeah, it's important to you to be a therapist, but can you accept you if others judge you negatively as a therapist? Can you accept Lottie?

[This does seem to be the core of Lottie's fear of being judged.]

Lottie: ... More lately, yes, I can. I'm starting to. I can see it breaking through.

Windy: The best way of doing that is to actually put it up there and then practise, rather than practise and then put it up there. Put it up there and say, 'OK, it's up there now. So, who do I think's gonna judge me? OK, this person that I fell out with. Well, what are they gonna say? OK, let's suppose they're saying it. OK, let me give them the right to say that. That's not nice, but let me practise accepting myself in the face of that. That's my armour. My self-acceptance is my protection. Not the perfection of the profile or the perfection of the website. The attitude of actually accepting me as a developing therapist going forward.'

[I like this response for a few reasons. First, I show that Lottie can put up her profile and website and then practise self-acceptance if she needs to rather than practise this attitude and then put up the material. Second, I show Lottie that self-acceptance can be her armour and by implication she doesn't need the armour of bullshit.]

Lottie: I can, yeah. I've only been seeing online clients, so it's kind of getting used to face to face again. So that's something. I wonder if that's added to it, yeah. I think I can. It feels like there's something breaking through.

Windy: OK, what's breaking through?

Lottie: A change of attitude. I think maybe it's because I'm moving as well. There's a whole sort of newness coming in. A sense of hope.

Windy: Was this course in Brentwood, ish?

Lottie: No, it was in Little Venice, in Paddington. CCPE, Paddington.

Windy: The Transpersonal.

Lottie: That's the one, yeah. So, I ended up getting a Master's. Not everybody did that either. So, I got the diploma, then the Master's.

Windy: So, you've worked pretty hard.

Lottie: Yeah.

Windy: It's important for you not to be a bullshitter, and that authenticity is important.

Lottie: Yeah.

Windy: But maybe you need to give people the right to be authentic in being critical of you and recognise that some of that might be projection but some of that might be because you've got unfinished business with certain people, that you need to bring to the table some self-acceptance.

Lottie: I might never even see them again.

Windy: That's not the point.

Lottie: Thinking about it, it's annoying.

Windy: That's not the point. You see them in your mind's eye.

Lottie: Yeah, I do.

Windy: And, therefore, I think you need to create a healthy reaction to any criticism that they have.

[*Notice, how I keep Lottie to the task of dealing with criticism from others.*]

Lottie: In my mind.

Windy: Yeah. If you did that, what difference do you think that would make to you?

Lottie: It would give me some space between me and them. I feel like they're here. This is obviously all in my mind. They're here and it would give me a little bit of space so they could move over and let me come in. I wouldn't have these eyes around me. It's not paranoia, but it's that kind of there's all eyes waiting to pounce.

Windy: Yeah. Is that how it felt like on the course?

Lottie: In the groupwork, yes. It did feel like that. It was difficult. Have you ever done groupwork?

Windy: I've done so much groupwork, it's not my thing, really.

Lottie: No, it's not my thing either, but it was interesting. I'm glad I did it. And sometimes you could feel a little bit like that with favourites. There were favourites on the course. I wasn't a favourite 'cos I was working full time, I didn't have the time to be there doing extra things. So, I didn't feel like I fitted into that posh – they're all quite wealthy, didn't have to work. So, I was very different.

Windy: Right, OK.

Lottie: But my old supervisor, she said, 'Well, use that. Say that you've worked in lots of different places, high-profile organisations, 'cos that can be something that you can bring to the table.'

Windy: It's almost like the way you describe them, there's an element of them looking down on you. Is that how it feels?

Lottie: … [*Pause*] Interesting, that, because it was difference. Privilege, that was the word. I don't know if I felt like they were looking down on me, because I did hold my own in terms of essays and I was able to keep up with everything, I did all my hours, got the UKCP, all of that. It was more of the have and have nots, the privilege, and then I don't feel like I was from a privileged background. It used to annoy me that they were able to just do the course and not have to work. There were a few others that were working as well, but you're dragging your arse into lectures.

Windy: Would you have liked to have had that privilege yourself?

Lottie: I'd like to have had less, maybe to have had the privilege of working part time. I don't think I'd want to not work at all. But it was good too, with the work, I was trying to think what I'd got from it that they might not have had. I was trying to look at – I don't know if that's the right way to do it.

Windy: It sounds like what you've got with what they didn't have is struggle strength: that you've struggled and you've come through.

[*Here, I highlight what Lottie has what these others don't have as a contrast to their 'privilege'.*]

Lottie: Yeah.

Windy: Whereas their privilege really protected them from struggling.

Lottie: That's true. And we were told working full time you're not going to be able to do that and complete this course, and I managed to do it.

Windy: You did, yeah.

Lottie: Yeah.

Windy: So maybe that is something that you can actually give yourself some credit for: that you've actually done something that it was predicted you couldn't go through. Yeah, it would've been nice to have some privilege, but you've actually done it the hard way and you've struggled and you've gone forward even though you've been struggling. And maybe that's the same thing that you can do with setting up your profile, your website and going forward, struggling forward.

[*Here, I am suggesting to Lottie that she can bring her 'struggle strength' to the task of creating her profile and website.*]

Lottie: Yeah, struggling.

Windy: But struggling not in the negative sense, but struggling in the sense that it's difficult. It's not easy putting up a profile. It's not easy doing a website. It's not easy setting up a full-time practice. It's a struggle. But you've got the wherewithal where you could struggle and go forward.

Lottie: Yeah, I can get through it.

Windy: And they haven't had that struggle.

Lottie: No.

Windy: You're privileged in the sense of having what they haven't had, in a way.

Lottie: OK. I'm just trying to think what that gives me over them. So, I've got a sense of aiming for something or struggling towards, going towards a goal.

Windy: If you believe in self-disclosure in therapy, with clients who struggle with struggling, so to speak, you can show them that you can struggle productively and achieve your goals, even though it's a struggle.

Lottie: Got you. I have had some clients that are in a similar position, actually, as well.... Yeah, I like that.

Windy: I mean, when I left the University of Aston, took voluntary redundancy back in 1983, and I was already a lecturer in counselling, and I went for jobs and I got rejected from 54 jobs, and I got a job on the 55th application. So, I had plenty of opportunity to deal with rejection, which was difficult, but I persisted and I developed the attitude that I had 54 job rejections and 0 self-rejections.

Lottie: That's like me when I was looking for a job in TV, and I got loads of rejection letters because I didn't know anyone. But then I did get a job in TV. So, it's a similar sort of thing. I kept all the letters.

Windy: If you bring that feistiness, you bring that ability to struggle forward and the positivity that comes out for that. You recognise that setting up a practice on your own and under difficult circumstances isn't easy, but, just because it isn't easy, you don't have to put it off. You can do what you've done already, which is struggle forward.

     [*Here, I am combining some of the positive qualities that Lottie has mentioned.*]

Lottie: Struggle forward. I like that. ... [*Pause*] Yeah, struggling forward.

     [*Lottie shows that she resonates with the term 'struggle forward'.*]

Windy: Because they haven't got that resilience. You've got that resilience that's come from struggling forward.

Lottie: That's the word, isn't it? Resilience. I think I wrote that on my form – resilience. There is a resilience about me.

[*And connecting it with resilience which Lottie remembers she put on her pre-session form.*]

Windy: You did.

Lottie: I do keep going. I don't get easily put off, normally.

Windy: So is there anything else that we need to talk about or is that going to help you to get a little unstuck going forward?

Lottie: Yeah, I think that's going to help me. That's good. So, what do I need to do? Do I need to write something up for you?

Windy: I will send you, in two months' time, a questionnaire in terms of your experience of today and what you made of it and what you've achieved as a result of it. And then we'll see where we go. You get to choose your name as well.

Lottie: Thank you, Windy. Really nice to meet you as well.

Windy: Nice to meet you.

Lottie's Follow-Up Questionnaire

Date: 25-03-25

Question	Response
1. What progress did you make on the issue that you brought to the session. Indicate the amount of progress you have made on this issue by using a 0% (no progress) – 100% (problem solved) scale.	**Issue Brought to the Session (Please name this):** I felt stuck in fully changing career. I completed my counselling and psychotherapy diploma in 2019 and gained my Masters and UKCP accreditation in 2021. I have a small practice alongside the day job but can't seem to make the leap into a full-time psychotherapy career. **Amount of progress made:** 70% **Factors that helped me make progress:** I now have more focus on the end goal. I have more clarity on the practical steps required, establishing a timeline and the mindset, ie, 'I need to struggle forward'. From next week, I will have an afternoon off from my day job each week to dedicate to therapy work. A small, but significant, step as I have worked full-time since the age of 22. I have also written the points to cover in my therapy directory entry.

	Factors that were absent that could have helped me make more progress: Time has been an issue as I have recently relocated and more of my spare time than usual has been taken up with the practicalities of that.
2. Did you make any progress on other issues that you have that you did not bring to our session? Please elaborate.	I have made small steps in some associated issues. These include considering what type of supervision I need moving forward and how working as a therapist fits into other aspects of my life.
3. How would you describe your relationship with Windy Dryden in the session?	I believe that a good rapport was established with Windy in a short space of time. This provided a good base from which to explore the issue.

4. What, if anything, did Windy Dryden do during the session that was helpful to you?	I was able to zoom in on the issue much quicker. Sometimes my mind can wander, and I can go off-track, but, in this session, I was very focused on the topic as I knew time was limited. I was also offered an external perspective, which allowed me to reflect and explore, from a different viewpoint.
5. What, if anything, did Windy Dryden do during the session that was unhelpful to you?	Nothing to really mention here. See point 10 for a more general comment around possible improvements.
6. How helpful did you find the pre-session form if you were sent one? Please elaborate.	The pre-session was helpful as it encouraged me to reflect and get to the heart of the issue. This helped to fend off lots of other thoughts coming in which can create diversions/blockers. The form reminded me of my journalism training. When you have a news story to write, with lots of information, we were challenged to imagine that you have just met a friend who you need to convey the core of the story to in around 25 words. This would be your introduction from which the rest of the story would flow.

7. How helpful did you find the audio-recording of your session? Please elaborate.	The recording was helpful as it allowed me to reflect back on the issue. Sometimes, in the moment, it can be difficult to remember all exchanges in the therapy room. As this was single-session therapy, following up for clarification is not as easy as with weekly sessions.
8. How helpful did you find the transcript of your sessions? Please elaborate.	The same as the above. The transcript also allowed me to go back on points even quicker than the audio-recording.
9. How does Single-Session Therapy compare with other therapies that you have had? Please elaborate.	Single-Session Therapy allows you to get to the heart of an issue with precise focus. A working rapport needs to be established between client and therapist much quicker. In contrast to this, the weekly therapy sessions I have previously had feel much slower, with a sense of something unfolding. There was more emphasis on the relationship between the therapist and myself in these sessions which became an important part of the work. In Single-Session Therapy, the focus is much more on the issue. I can, however, see similarities with a single-session hypnotherapy session I had, which worked on one particular issue.

10. What improvements, if any, do you think need to be made to the Single-Session Therapy framework?	If needed, it would be helpful to spend a little more time at the end of the session, or build in time following the session, to direct the client to other sources of support (ie, books, media).
11. Please give any additional feedback that your responses to the questions above have not covered.	I found the session really useful – it offered an interesting perspective on a therapeutic approach I knew little about. I can now share this information with therapy colleagues and clients, where appropriate.

My Reflections and Summary

On her pre-session form, Lottie stated that she wanted to discuss the stuckness she experiences making a full career change. Her goal was to find a path towards making that change. In her follow-up questionnaire, Lottie said that she made 70% progress on the 0–100% progress scale . She said that she now has more focus on the end goal. She has more clarity on the practical steps requiring, establishing a timeline and the mindset, i.e., 'I need to struggle forward'. She plans to have an afternoon off from my day job each week to dedicate to therapy work. A small, but significant, step as she has worked full-time since the age of 22. I had also written the points to cover in my therapy directory entry. In other areas of her life, Lottie made small steps in some associated issues. These included considering what type of supervision she needed moving forward and how working as a therapist fits into other aspects of my life.

I thought that my work with Lottie was basically good although I needed to be more explicit with her about her session goals We were able to focus and remain focused on the factors that explained her stuckness and what Lottie can do to respond to these factors. I was able to help Lottie bring to the issue some of her strengths that she was able to incorporate into her plan.

In terms of our therapeutic relationship, Lottie said that a good rapport was established with me in a short space of time. This provided a good base from which to explore the issue. Concerning what was helpful in the session, Lottie said she was able to zoom in on the issue quite quickly. She said that sometimes her mind can wander, and she can go off-track, but, in this session, she was very focused on the topic as she knew time was limited.

Regarding the pre-session form, recording, and transcript, Lottie mentioned the following. She found the pre-session form helpful as it encouraged her to reflect and get to the heart of the issue. This, she said, helped to fend off lots of other thoughts coming in which can create diversions/blockers.

Lottie said that the both the recording and transcript were helpful as they allowed her to reflect back on the issue, more quickly in the case of the transcript. As she said, sometimes, in the moment, it can be difficult to remember all exchanges in the therapy room. As this was single-session therapy, following up for clarification is not as easy as with weekly sessions.

9

Dealing with Stuck Feelings of Anger Towards My Mother

Date: 28-01-25
Time: 38 mins 14 secs

Helen's Pre-Session Form

Helen said that she wanted to discuss her feelings of anger towards her mother as she ages and has more needs. She added that growing up many of her own emotional needs were not met and the role reversal is triggering. Her goal from the session was to get unstuck enough with some of the anger that she doesn't have regrets about how she has acted. The steps that she has taken to deal with this issue were therapy, meditation and developing self-compassion. Helen said her strengths were resilience and that she uses meditation to self-regulate.

The Session

Windy: So, Helen, what's your understanding of the purpose of our conversation today?

Helen: I mean, I suppose just that it's the opportunity for me to experience single-session therapy and about trying to get a little bit unstuck with something I'm struggling with.

Windy: So, you still want to be stuck but you want to be a little unstuck?

Helen: Well, maybe I've just got realistic expectations. If you could do better than that, that would be amazing.

Windy: Well, maybe *we* can do better than that.

   [*In this response, I am pointing out that this is a 'we' task, not a 'me' task.*]

Helen: OK.

Windy: So why don't you put it into your own words what you are stuck with, and then we can see what being unstuck looks like for you? Let's start with the stuckness. What are you stuck with?

   [*In this response, I indicate that I want to understand Helen's issue with stuckness but by alluding to what being unstuck looks like for her, I am suggesting that things can be different and that I can help her move towards a state of unstuckness.*]

Helen: I am stuck with feeling, I suppose, a lot of feelings of anger and just feeling quite triggered when I'm around my mother. I mean, my mother, she's going to be 80 this year and I suppose her needs are getting a lot greater now and I'm just feeling really triggered by what feels like a real role reversal in terms of meeting her needs when it feels like my needs were not seen a great deal when I was younger.

Windy: Could you tell me who was in your family growing up so I can put this into a wider context?

Helen: OK. So, I am one of four sisters. I'm the youngest. So, my older sister is a good bit older than me. So, she moved out of the house when I was about five or six. Then my mother and father were together, they separated when I was about 13. I did have a grandmother. She died maybe the year before that, but all my other grandparents had already passed away by the time I was born. I mean, I've got lots of extended family, but that's the family unit.

Windy: And what needs of yours weren't met when you were growing up?

Helen: … I'd say more my emotional needs. I mean, my mother and father split up when I was, like I said, around 13 and my father moved away and had very little involvement after that time. Later in life we reconnected, but throughout my childhood he wasn't around.

And my mum was a single mother. She did the best she could in the sense that she provided for me and my next sister up – we were still living at home at the time. And she met the physical needs. There was food, we had shelter, we had those kinds of needs. But, when it came to emotional needs, she's very emotionally immature.

Windy: Meaning what, Helen?

Helen: Meaning she really struggles to see things from somebody else's perspective. It's very much from her perspective and really lacks insight into recognising that somebody else might have different feelings to her. So, everything was from her perspective. I can give examples of that.

Windy: No, I get the picture. Do your other sisters feel the same way as you do?

Helen: My two older sisters don't really have contact with her. The next sister up feels very similar to me, yeah.

Windy: But the ones that don't have any contact with her now, do they feel as well that she never met their emotional needs?

Helen: Yeah.

Windy: OK. So, she didn't have favourites. She didn't meet anybody's emotional needs growing up, because it sounds like, from your description, she saw things very much from her point of view and was really not able very easily to see things from your point of view.

Helen: Yeah.

Windy: So that's a useful context for me to understand. What's going on now, then?

[*I often find it useful to understand the context of a problem like the one Helen has described. In this case, I will keep in mind that Helen's mother struggled to meet any of her daughters' emotional needs because she viewed life solely from her own perspective and couldn't consider her daughters' viewpoints.*]

Helen: In the relationship between us now?

Windy: Yeah. You said that you're stuck and you're triggered, and I want to understand that a little bit more.

Helen: Well, I suppose now when I'm around her I just feel like she's regressed so much that she is very demanding of her needs, and it feels very in my face. And I suppose I have worked very hard over the years to validate myself and allow myself to have needs, and it feels like now when I'm in her company and everything is about her needs, there's a part of me, I don't know, not willing to abandon myself in the relationship with her. But I feel really angry.

Windy: Towards?

Helen: Towards her.

Windy: For?

Helen: For not seeing me. For not seeing me and for her needs to be so at the forefront. It's almost like... I resent having to take on the role of being the carer when it feels like my needs were not seen.

Windy: Right. Does she live with you?

Helen: No. I suppose just to get a little bit more context, we live quite a distance apart from each other, like 400 miles, so, when we do spend time with each other, it's staying in each other's houses. So, it's very intense.

Windy: How long for?

Helen: Well, for example, just there we were a combination of staying at her house and my house four weeks.

Windy: Right, OK. And what about your other sister, does she take turns as well?

Helen: She does, yeah.

Windy: She has the same feelings as you do of anger?

Helen: Yeah.

Windy: In your pre-session form, I wanted to clarify because I wasn't sure whether you were regretting the feeling of anger or the behaviour about how you acted. In response to the question, 'What is your goal in discussing this issue in the session with me?' you said, 'To get unstuck enough from some of the anger that I don't have regrets about how I have acted.'

              [*Having understood the context, I decided to refer to Helen's pre-session form to clarify her goal for the session, as I was uncertain about what she wanted from it.*]

Helen: Yeah. I mean, I feel really impatient with her. I'm not acting or being aggressive or anything, but I am really impatient with her.

Windy: How do you manage your impatience so that there's no behavioural manifestation of that impatience, it sounds like?

Helen: How do I manage it? I mean, I probably do express my frustration. ... I suppose I dig my heels in a little bit. If she is asking for something to take place and it's very much from her perspective, I will dig my heels in and I try to show what I need in those situations as well. That I am very impatient in the way that I respond to her.

Windy: How would you like to respond to her at that point?

Helen: ... [Pause] I don't know. This is where I feel stuck because part of me feels like I'm not going to abandon myself in situations, but I would like to feel less angry.

Windy: So, it sounds like there's two things going on: you feel stuck and you don't have a clear vision of what being unstuck is like.

Helen: Maybe being unstuck is me being able to find the balance between... keeping my needs in the mix – if I'm able to have some kind of compromise where both of our needs can be met, but that, I don't know, that I don't feel as triggered, that I don't feel as angry. So, it's like I've been trying to think about the way she did meet my needs in other ways to try and see if that helps with reducing my anger.

[I think it would have been better to have gotten greater clarity from Helen on what

*she hoped for by the end of the session.
Aiming to be less angry is confusing.*]

Windy: What other ways have you tried to do that?

Helen: Reflecting on the way she did meet my needs, the way that she stayed when my father didn't.

Windy: Right. How capable do you think she is of being able to not see things from her point of view and see things from other people's point of view? How capable do you think she is of doing that?

Helen: … Well, is it capable, or is it just not trying?

Windy: I don't know.

Helen: I don't know.

Windy: What it sounds like, she's just never done it, and she's not doing it now. If I can piece together some of the things that I'm hearing that seem to be relevant is that one is the reality of her, which is a person who is what you call emotionally immature, you spell out what that means and that is seeing everything from her point of view and not seeing other people's point of view. That seems to be a component of it. And the importance of you not giving up yourself. And I'm wondering if you're clear with yourself about what you are prepared to do for her and what you're not prepared to do for her.

[Again, a focus on Helen's session goal would have been better here.]

Helen: ... [*Pause*] Maybe I could be clearer. I know that recently she made it clear that there were expectations from her that she would have liked to have moved in with either myself or my sister, and I'm clear that that wouldn't work.

Windy: How did you express that?

Helen: Well, it was actually my sister who expressed that in the end.

Windy: If it was you, how would you have done it?

Helen: I would be saying that it just wouldn't work, in the sense of it would cause a ripple effect in my family life, and that wouldn't work.

Windy: So, if it was down to you, you could imagine telling her that, 'No, it's not gonna happen and this is the reason why it's not gonna happen.'

Helen: Yeah.

Windy: What would you expect from her in response?

Helen: What would I like or what would I expect?

Windy: Well, what would you like?

Helen: I would like her to have a level of understanding about that.

Windy: And what would you expect?

Helen: Not to. Victim mode, probably.

Windy: And how would you respond to that victim mode?

Helen: Probably with frustration.

Windy: Why?

Helen: … Because I'm not being seen or understood.

Windy: Well, you see, that's the thing, isn't it? It's true, you're not, but there are two ends to that statement that you're not providing for yourself, it seems to me, in my view. Do you want to hear what that is? 'I'm not being seen'. One is 'I'm not going to be seen because this is my mother. She doesn't have that capacity or the willingness or whatever it is. She doesn't do that.' And the other thing, 'Sadly, regretfully and somewhat tragically, I don't have to be seen.'

Helen: ... [*Long pause*] I don't know, though, I feel like I really need that.

Windy: From whom?

Helen: ... [*Long pause*] Well, I suppose I needed it from her.

Windy: Yes, and I think partly it is that there's still a part of you that hasn't given up hope that the final analysis, the cavalry comes just when the Indians are about to attack. I think you're touched by that because I think that is something. It's what I call the 'cod liver oil moment', which is swallowing that and saying, 'Look, unfortunately, even at the last minute it's not gonna happen because this is my mother we're talking about.' And that's the sadness. What I'm hearing is sadness. Maybe if you can get in touch with the sadness rather than the anger and the regret, that might help you.

Helen: I think the regret, it is more about, like I said, time is of the essence and I know it's not infinite here. And the only bit that I can control here is how I act. But there is a sadness there and I suppose the reality is I don't feel comfortable being vulnerable around my mother and it doesn't feel OK to show my sadness there.

Windy: What would she do if you did? Do you mean show it on your face or talk about or what?

Helen: … Both of those things.

Windy: Well, look, I think that everybody in life comes with a user manual, like fridges do. So, your user manual is extraordinarily different from your mother's user manual, it sounds to me like. And her user manual is almost saying, 'This unit only sees things from its perspective no matter who it is. She may love, she may express love through physical means, but this unit does not express things through emotional means.' And I don't know what she's like at responding to emotionality, but what I'm hearing is that you see sadness as a vulnerability.

Helen: In that relationship.

Windy: Yeah, but, in a way, sadness is about the realisation, in this case, of loss and the even sadder realisation that that need is not going to be met. And, so, if you could allow yourself to be sad, but, as I say, there's no point in saying that because all she'll do is turn it around. But, if you allow yourself to feel sad in your own time, in your own way, I'm just wondering if you can incorporate that into the whole picture, what that would do for you.

Helen: I feel like I have learnt so well to push these emotions down, especially in that relationship.... I, by default, seem to move to anger. It feels safer.

Windy: Yeah. Anger is powerful. Sadness is vulnerable, let's say. There are different types of anger. There's one which is saying, 'This is a pain in the arse, but, sadly, it is what it is. It doesn't have to be different,' and the kind of anger that says, 'No, it has to be different. Because I didn't get it, why should I give it 'cos I didn't get it?' and that kind of thing. All I'm saying is not all angers are the same. I'm wondering if you could develop the kind of anger which is gonna be really understandable, it's a response again to the idea of the unfairness of the situation that you are expected to give something that you didn't get.

[This is the first time I talk about there being different 'angers'. Can Helen find the kind of anger that is acceptable to her? Since it is unlikely that she is not going to feel any anger.]

Helen: Yeah.

Windy: But you don't have to give it. You're choosing to give it, don't forget.

Helen: Yeah, and I am. And, like I said, while a part of me is very clear about moving in is not ever gonna happen ... to me I feel like it's really important that I can give her what I can. For example, I would offer if she wanted to move closer to me. I would be available to help her out in the ways that I could. But my line is very clear on moving in is not gonna work.

Windy: That's right, and I think, if you bring that determination to the little things and really see what you're prepared to do and what you're not prepared to do, to get in touch with the unfairness type of anger but to recognise that you have a choice. You don't have to do things, you're choosing to do things, and I think you're choosing to do things out of love. And I think the biggest thing for you to take, and this is a two-spoon cod liver, in my view the cavalry's never gonna come, Helen, and that's really sad. But maybe you don't need the cavalry anymore. It would be nice to have, but maybe you have enough in your life going for you.

Helen: Yeah. I mean, I do. The other side of it is I am cultivating a life that has got a lot more meaning and nurturing relationships, and I know that. But there's still this kind of yearning there, I suppose.

Windy: Yearning for what?

Helen: Well, to be nurtured, to have a kind of mother–daughter relationship, even though my logical mind knows that's not gonna happen.

Windy: OK. So enough of this counselling rubbish. I'm gonna give it to you. Do you see this?

Helen: Hmm mmm [yes].

Windy: What is it?

Helen: A magic wand.

Windy: That's right. None of this counselling. We're gonna wave that and when you go home you'll find that your mother will be very different, à la Dryden. What's the chances?

Helen: Yeah, it's not gonna happen.

Windy: No, and that's the bit that you need to come to terms with. And I think all the rest of it is secondary, really. But it is unfair. Human beings go for reciprocity. You're basically saying, 'Well, why should give it to her? She never gave it to me. I'm not gonna reciprocate.' It's almost like saying, 'Well, now I'm giving it to her, I expect her to give it to me,' again the reciprocity. And that works with people who are flexible. Your mother on this issue isn't.

[*I think I missed an opportunity to acknowledge the part of Helen that still yearns for her mother to meet her emotional needs and do some work with that part of her.*]

Helen: I know, and there is an element, when you asked that question about how capable is she, and I'll give you an example – I've been and studied and graduated on a few different occasions and never ever once has she said to me she's proud for what I've achieved or anything. But on one of my graduations she did sit and speak to my husband and tell him she was proud of what I've done. So, there's an element of she can see that.

Windy: Sure. I think there has to be put into a generational context as well. I think my father was the same. He never said he was proud of me directly, but he used to say to other people that he was proud of me. So, I just thought, 'Well, OK, I'm getting the message second-hand. It would be nice to get it first-hand.' So, I think maybe you're gonna get it second-hand rather than first-hand.

Helen: Well, that was probably a rare occasion that that took place.

Windy: Well, I don't know how much time you spend eavesdropping on what she says about you, but you never know. There is that dynamic. There's that embarrassment of actually saying that directly which may be a factor. I don't know.

Helen: I suppose I just don't understand that because I can't praise my children enough, and it's hard for me to see it from that perspective.

Windy: Well, that's it, isn't it? If she was a client, not a relation to you, and she was somebody who really came in and said, 'Well, I put food on the table, I made sure that everybody was clean,' and things like that, and you say, 'What about your child's emotional needs?' and she said, 'Nope, I don't do that,' would you find it hard to empathise with that person in a counselling context?

Helen: ... [*Pause*] I would probably be able to see the bigger picture easier.

Windy: And what would the bigger picture be?

Helen: ... That she was born just after the war and that her parents were probably very much in threat mode and did very little of the emotional stuff when she was growing up. I would see that ... she's done the things she could in the sense of practical things. She did hang around and be a single parent. And I would be able to see that and maybe be able to hold onto those other things. But it's easier not from a personal perspective.

304   *Single-Session Therapy and Getting Unstuck*

Windy: Well, yeah, I know, because, when you put the personal perspective, what do you add to that?

Helen: Well, the hurt of what it feels like in the absence of those things.

[This is another indication that I have failed to address what I now think is the core of Helen's issue – working with the hurt part of her who still yearns for her mother to acknowledge and meet her emotional needs.]

Windy: Yeah. So, I think there's a number of components here which makes this complex. One is the idea that there's a context for her, that she was probably not given any emotional needs herself, therefore she found it difficult to actually give. It didn't stop you. In fact, in a way, we could look at this that you broke the legacy and passed on a very different legacy to your children. And that, yeah, when you factor in you, because it's you and there's not an unreasonable expectation that parents ideally should meet one's emotional needs, but we know that in actuality a lot don't, and yours is included in that. Therefore, that is hurtful and sad, and you have a choice about how much of what you do, and you're quite clear you ain't gonna let her live with you 'cos therein lies masochism, it seems to me. So, you are drawing the line there. You can draw the line in other areas, recognising that you can be sad and healthily angry. The unhealthy anger is rigid, saying, 'Because it's unfair, it must not be this way.' Well, maybe on the Planet Helen it wouldn't be, but on the Planet Earth this is what we've got to play with.

Helen: Yeah.

Windy: So, your job is to bring all those things together. That's complicated.

Helen: Yeah. And, while that might be the dialogue playing out in my head, it's not what I'm saying to her, screaming about the unfairness of things. I mean, it might be what I'm screaming in my head.

Windy: So maybe you need to have a word with you first. Maybe you need to prepare yourself a little bit when you think that you might get into that internal screaming first. You may be saying, 'What's gonna happen now is my mother's gonna ignore my emotional needs. Well, how am I gonna deal with that? What are my choices?' and recognise you do have choices.

Helen: Yeah. ... Yeah, and I suppose that's why I put on the form around maybe let go of some of the anger enough, because I'm realistic enough to know that maybe the anger is speaking from that part of me that cares more about my needs now and it is that sense of injustice there.

Windy: Yeah, and I think just recognise that there is a part of you, a part of all of us, and that part of us is saying, 'It shouldn't be this way.' So, you could either continue with that or you say, 'Well, yeah, but it is this way,' whether it should or shouldn't. So, you recognise that there is that part of you that also needs to be understood. But you can prepare yourself. Do you know when this dynamic is likely to play out? Can you predict it?

[My work on Helen's anger is largely informed by the REBT concept of anger being underpinned by a rigid attitude. I wished I been more open to her about this. Also, I wish I had explored the connection more between hurt and anger. If Helen did not feel hurt about her mother not meeting her emotional needs, what impact would that have on her anger?]

Helen: In what sense?

Windy: That you pretty much know that you're going to go into a situation and your mother's gonna ignore your needs and just put her needs to the fore?

Helen: Can I predict that? That's how it'll play out pretty much.

Windy: So, what I'm saying is you can prepare for that.

Helen: Yeah.

Windy: How would you prepare for it to your satisfaction?

Helen: … [*Pause*] I mean, I suppose maybe getting more clear about what I need in situations. … [*Pause*] I mean, there are certain things which are obvious to me but there are probably things on smaller levels that I could be clearer about. … [*Pause*] I mean, I don't know, I suppose I spend a lot of time creating a lot of busyness in my life and that leaves me feeling quite stressed a lot of the time. So, trying to be there, about not being so busy if I know I'm going to be in her company, slowing things down a little bit.

Windy: Yeah. But I'm talking about the psychological preparation that you need to do in terms of attitude or framework that you need to hold onto during the interaction with her.

Helen: I suppose just keeping it really basic around that reminder to myself that… [*pause*] I'm not gonna get what I need in those situations and almost being able to find a way of letting go of that expectation, because, yeah, my adult self knows that that's not coming, but that reminder that… it isn't coming.

Windy: Yeah, and the recognition that that is sad, don't forget that, and that you can acknowledge that kind of sadness. It's a bit like my mother every day used to cry over losing her mother. She used to do that regularly. And I said, 'Are you upset about this?' and she said, 'No, every day I just remember my mother and have a little cry and then I get on with things.' So maybe you could have a little cry and get on with things while recognising that it is sad, because we don't want you to repress that. We don't want you to ignore that. But I think, if you can get in touch with that and recognise that maybe you can take a little sip of the cod liver oil bit by bit. I talked about swallowing a couple of spoonfuls, but that's looking at it as a whole. But, when you're doing it over time, recognising that, 'It is sad that my mother's like this.'

[*Here I stress that it is important that Helen acknowledge her sadness, and also her hurt feelings which I have argued are also present in the totality of her experience with anger.*]

Helen: Yeah, and I suppose I soften a little when I can connect with the sadness.

Windy: Yeah. And, when you soften a little, what happens to your interactions with her?

Helen: … [*Pause*] I suppose … [*pause*] the more that I'm not in that angry place, the more that I'm able to connect with sadness, then, I don't know, I probably feel less frustrated with her then and I'm maybe more connected to … I don't know, my sadness. It's maybe a little bit more reflecting on me as opposed to her.

Windy: Yeah. 'Cos, in a way, the difference between the sadness that she never gave it to you, but also the sadness that you never got it. In a way, the way I would look at it is that you broke the legacy, because you could've passed on the same thing.

Helen: Don't get me wrong, I'm sure I'll give my kids reasons to go to therapy themselves. It'll be different reasons, I hope.

Windy: Yeah, I'm sure it'll be different reasons. What I'm saying is it sounds like, from what you were saying, that you learnt that it was really important to meet your kids' emotional needs.

Helen: Yeah.

Windy: The way I look at it, your mother was a good teacher about what not to do.

Helen: Yep.... I think that's just as powerful a lesson.

Windy: Yeah, indeed. So, what's gonna be the takeaways for you, Helen, from this consultation?

Helen: ... I don't know. I suppose that ... just that reinforcement of ... it isn't coming. I need to remind that part of me that still yearns for it that it isn't coming, because I think it is still battling in some way to want to receive it. So that reminder that this really isn't coming, and I suppose, as I watch her age, that's becoming clearer. Maybe there's more of a fight in me because of that. But the other thing, I suppose, is ... [*pause*] just connecting to the sadness, because I can easily default to the anger, but connecting to the sadness of it.

Windy: And I think you can do that in advance of meeting with her. So, I think connect with the sadness a little bit, have a little internal weep if you need to and soften up and then take that, Helen, into the interaction, and let's see what happens.

Helen: Yeah.

Windy: Is there anything that you want to say that you haven't said or anything you want to ask that you haven't asked that you might regret not asking or saying when we've finished?

Helen: ... Not that I can think of right now, no. Thank you.

Windy: I will send you the recording and later the transcript. In two months, I'll send you an evaluation form for you to fill out, and it'll be interesting to see what you make of this.

Helen: Yeah. And I suppose the only other thing is just around anonymising things.

Windy: Yeah. When you get the transcript, if you want to just highlight in yellow the bits you want me to omit. And what I will do is I will ask you to come up with an alternative name.

Helen: OK. Later for that?

Windy: Yeah. I want to give you some time to think about that.

Helen's Follow-Up Questionnaire

Date: 26 March 2025

Question	Response
1. What progress did you make on the issue that you brought to the session. Indicate the amount of progress you have made on this issue by using a 0% (no progress) – 100% (problem solved) scale.	**Issue Brought to the Session (Please name this):** Stuckness in my relationship with my mother. Having expectations that she would see me more. **Amount of progress made:** 50% **Factors that helped me make progress:** The directness of the therapist helped me get perspective around the likelihood of change, it highlighted that if it has been this way all my life, the chances of it changing in my mother's later stage of life, are highly unlikely. I needed that challenge. This helped me move from anger and touch grief. **Factors that were absent that could have helped me make more progress:** I can't think of any. I have been stuck with this issue for many years and spoke repeatedly in therapy about it.

2. Did you make any progress on other issues that you have that you did not bring to our session? Please elaborate.	I didn't discuss any issues outside of the above listed.
3. How would you describe your relationship with Windy Dryden in the session?	Direct, yet warm enough to hold the directness. I expected it to be that way given its SST. However, I was unsure how it would feel, but in some ways it felt quite trusting in me, trusting that I could hear it. I liked that.
4. What, if anything, did Windy Dryden do during the session that was helpful to you?	The magic wand was helpful, and directly challenging me in terms of my expectations that change would in any way be likely.
5. What, if anything, did Windy Dryden do during the session that was unhelpful to you?	Nothing came up. The time was short.
6. How helpful did you find the pre-session form if you were sent one? Please elaborate.	I found the pre-session form helpful to consolidate my thoughts before attending. Without it I could have spent the hour trying to create a context. It helped me be concise and prepared for attending.

7. How helpful did you find the audio-recording of your session? Please elaborate.	I didn't re-watch the video, I find it hard to watch myself on video.
8. How helpful did you find the transcript of your sessions? Please elaborate.	It was helpful to re-read over the dialogue.
9. How does Single-Session Therapy compare with other therapies that you have had? Please elaborate.	I liked the directness. With that said, if I hadn't done many hours of other therapy around the issue previously, I'm not sure how I would have felt about it then. The fact it was focusing on something stuck worked really well.
10. What improvements, if any, do you think need to be made to the Single-Session Therapy framework?	I can't think of anything that would improve it.
11. Please give any additional feedback that your responses to the questions above have not covered.	Overall experiencing SST has made me curious to learn more about the approach.

My Reflections and Summary

On her pre-session form, Helen stated that she wanted to discuss the stuckness she experienced concerning her angry feelings towards her mother. Her goal was to find a way to get unstuck. In her follow-up questionnaire, Helen said that she made 50% progress on the 0%-100% progress scale. She said that the following factors helped her to make progress. My directness as a therapist helped her to gain perspective around the likelihood of change. It highlighted that if it has been this way all her life, and helped her to acknowledge that the chances of it changing in her mother's later stage of life were highly unlikely. Helen said that she needed that challenge. It helped her move from anger and touch grief.

I thought that my work with Helen was adequate but lacking in several respects. While the work was sufficiently focused, it lacked sufficient goal direction. I also think that I did not get to the heart of the matter, which would have involved dealing with that part of Helen that still yearned to have her emotional needs met by her mother, even though from a realistic perspective this was not going to happen. While I identified and worked with Helen's sadness/grief, I did not identify and work with her feelings of hurt which as I see it now lay underneath her anger towards her mother. Now, I may be in error about this, but I wished that I had created the opportunity of discussing it with Helen.

Having thought about this, I decided to send the above paragraph to Helen for her comments. This is what she said:

'Thanks for sharing your thoughts on the session. I'm not so sure about the idea of it being "insufficiently goal-directed" – I actually experienced it as quite direct, in a helpful way. The angry part of me really needed to hear that what I yearn for – being emotionally met – isn't coming. That was hard, but it helped something shift, as you said, into a more useful kind of anger. A more accepting kind. The kind that says, *yes*, I was right to be angry … and *it is what it is*.

'I think you're right that there's hurt underneath. It's been pushed down for so long as a form of self-protection that it can feel almost out of reach. Maybe that part of me would have benefited from being seen more clearly in the room, although reading back over the transcript and your reflections did bring a tear to my eye. Your noticing of that hurt part now helps it feel a little more seen and validated. So – thank you!'

In terms of our therapeutic relationship, Helen said that it was direct, yet warm enough to hold the directness. She expected it to be that way given it is SST. However, she was unsure how it would feel, but in some ways it felt quite trusting in her, trusting that she could hear what I had to say. She liked that. Helen specifically referenced the magic wand that I waved in the session as being was helpful in directly challenging her in terms of her expectations that change would in any way be likely.

Regarding the pre-session form, recording, and transcript, Helen mentioned the following. She found the pre-session form helpful to consolidate her thoughts before attending. Without it, she said that she could have spent the hour trying to create a context. It helped her be concise and prepared for attending. Helen said she did not watch the video. She was not aware that I sent her the audio recording of the session, not the video. She did read the transcript, which she found helpful.

10

Afterword

In this book, I have presented eight single-sessions that I conducted with volunteers who wanted help with an emotional issue with which they felt stuck. When I give training sessions on SST, people new to single-session therapy ask several questions and the following are relevant to the work described in this book and can thus be answered.

Do People Benefit from a Single Session?

Other therapists often want to know what benefit can a person derive from a single session of therapy. Two to three months after the sessions all participants reported that they had made between 50% and 80% progress using a 0–100% progress scale. I think this shows that while a single-session is frequently insufficient to lead a person to get completely unstuck from an issue with which they have felt stuck, it can lead to a significant amount of change. On the basis of these findings, I would be happy for SST to be promoted as a way of helping a person begin the process of getting unstuck on a stuck issue.

What Issues Do People Bring to SST?

The range of issues that people reported in this book brought to SST was quite wide – criticism, unrequited love, betrayal, rejection, self-doubt and fear of failure, co-dependency, making a full career change and anger. This shows that SST therapists can take an open access approach to helping people who come for help when they feel stuck with an emotional issue.

How Long Is a Session?

I am often asked how long does a single session last for. In my own practice I say to clients that I will see them for *up to* 50 minutes. In this book the conversations ranged from: 34 minutes 25 seconds to 48 minutes – well within the usual 50 minutes that most therapists allocate to a session. As I often say the work determines the length of a single session, not the clock.

Can You Develop a Good Therapeutic Relationship in a Single Session?

The question that I get asked most frequently about SST is this: 'Can you develop a good enough therapeutic relationship in SST?' (Dryden, 2022). The best way to answer this question is to let the volunteers in this book speak for themselves. In their follow-up questionnaire, they were asked the following question: 'How would you describe your relationship with Windy Dryden in the session?' Here are their responses:

- 'Windy created a welcoming and safe space, I felt he asked the right questions to build a picture and explore why I was reacting with fear of rejection when experiencing criticism' (Sarah Louise, Chapter 2).

- 'I found Windy to be warm, knowledgeable and challenging without being directly critical. I would describe our relationship as being fluid and yet boundaried at the same time' (Ruth, Chapter 3).
- I was aware of his warmth but also his clear boundaries and directive approach, which is key to single-session therapy. I felt very clearly seen and understood within the session by Windy (Cat, Chapter 4).
- 'I felt it was easy to work with Windy, having a shared goal and understanding of the process helped me feel like we were working together towards an outcome/resolution' (Sylvia, Chapter 5).
- 'Excellent. Windy has a lovely relaxed personality that instantly helps to make others feel relaxed, I enjoyed the way he explained certain thoughts' (Louise, Chapter 6).
- 'I believe Windy and I formed a connection relatively quickly during our session. I sensed a warm and trusting dynamic between us, and I felt genuinely heard and understood' (Lily, Chapter 7).
- 'I believe that a good rapport was established with Windy in a short space of time. This provided a good base from which to explore the issue' (Lottie, Chapter 8).
- 'Direct, yet warm enough to hold the directness. I expected it to be that way given its SST. However, I was unsure how it would feel, but in some ways it felt quite trusting in me, trusting that I could hear it. I liked that' (Helen, Chapter 9).

Irving Yalom recently published a book of his single-session consultations in which he discussed single sessions with people which he conducted based on the well-known principle that 'it is the relationship that heals' (Yalom and Yalom, 2024). I critiqued this work and highlighted the conundrums that arise from applying this principle too literally in single-session work (Dryden, 2025b). What the responses from volunteers in this book show is the importance of developing a good enough therapeutic relationship so that the often challenging work of helping people to get unstuck can be done. My own view on the role of the therapeutic relationship in SST echoes Lottie's experience of her relationship with me (see above). My task in SST is to build a strong rapport with someone quickly. Doing so provides a secure base from which to explore the issue and help the person achieve their hoped-for outcome from the session.

What Do People Find Helpful and Unhelpful About Single Sessions?

Feedback from volunteers on their follow-up questionnaires indicated that, overall, participants felt the session was beneficial for them. I will expand on this in two ways. First, I will provide volunteers' responses to the request for them to consider, 'Factors that helped me make progress'. Second, I will provide volunteers' responses to the question, 'What, if anything, did Windy Dryden do during the session that was helpful to you?'

Factors that Helped Volunteers Progress

Volunteers considered the following helped them to progress. After each statement, I will speculate which therapeutic factor this exemplified.

- 'Thinking of how feeling criticised doesn't have to evoke a strong emotional response. If it is true, then it's only a criticism of a part of me and it doesn't have to be all consuming' (Sarah Louise, Chapter 2) – *New Learning*

- 'Acknowledging that my time is precious and my personal boundaries are important. Assisting me to understand that my repeated patterns of behaviour within relationships were caused by me not wanting to enter into conflict with my partners, which led to my own suffering' (Ruth, Chapter 3) – *New Learning*

- 'Accepting that much was outside of my control and that I might not find what I am longing for somehow enabled me to begin to hold the issue less defensively/more open-mindedly (Cat, Chapter 4) – *Acceptance*

- 'Breaking down the issue, recognising the different types of hurt I was experiencing' (Sylvia, Chapter 5) – *New Learning*

- 'Looking at the issues that I felt stuck with, and reframing them as if the decision was taken out of my control' (Louise, Chapter 6) – *Reframing*

- 'With Windy's advice, I have slowed down a lot in terms of getting to know people first before leaping in. I have realised the importance of being friends with someone rather than jump straight into a relationship before we know each other well' (Lily, Chapter, 7) – **Behaviour Change**

- 'I now have more focus on the end goal. I have more clarity on the practical steps required, establishing a timeline and the mindset, i.e., 'I need to struggle forward'. From next week, I will have an afternoon off from my day job each week to dedicate to therapy work. A small, but significant, step as I have worked full-time since the age of 22. I have also written the points to cover in my therapy directory entry' (Lottie, Chapter 8) – **Becoming Goal-Directed and Behaviour Change**

- 'The directness of the therapist helped me get perspective around the likelihood of change, it highlighted that if it has been this way all my life, the chances of it changing in my mother's later stage of life, are highly unlikely. I needed that challenge. This helped me move from anger and touch grief' (Helen, Chapter 9) – **Acceptance**

What Windy Dryden Did in the Session that Was Helpful to Volunteers

Volunteers said the following concerning what I did in the session that was helpful to them:

- 'Challenged my perspective to help me reframe' (Sarah Louise, Chapter 2) – **Reframing**

- 'Windy gave another perspective on my issues that were not yet in my awareness. My friends now carry a red flag in their handbags to alert me to unsuitable dating choices' (Ruth, Chapter 3) – *Reframing*

- 'Close to the end of the session, Windy said that he had not heard anything that made him think anything other than what I wanted was possible for me. I found that reassuring and a positive antidote to the shame I have always carried around this issue' (Cat, Chapter 4) – *Validation*

- 'He explained things clearly and concisely' (Sylvia, Chapter 5) – *Clarity*

- 'Windy helped me look at my situation through a different lens' (Louise, Chapter 6) – *Reframing*

- 'I found Windy's humour uplifting and helped removed a great deal of judgement and anger towards myself that I have been carrying since my last breakup. He encouraged me to have some self-compassion in the same way I would towards a friend. I have noticed a lot of change in this area. I found him waving the red flag hilarious. I also found his comment that he doesn't think this is coming from a deep insecurity really interesting and one I hadn't considered before. I always had assumed it must be something buried deep down, which it may be, but I agree that it's more to do with an intense attraction to the 'high' and euphoria of love (Lily, Chapter 7) – *Humour and Self-Compassion*

- 'I was able to zoom in on the issue much quicker. Sometimes my mind can wander, and I can go off-track, but, in this session, I was very focused on the topic as I knew time was limited. I was also offered an external perspective, which allowed me to reflect and explore, from a different viewpoint' (Lottie, Chapter 8) – **Focus and Reframing**

- 'The magic wand was helpful, and directly challenging me in terms of my expectations that change would in any way be likely' (Helen, Chapter 9) – **Humour and Challenge**

Other Issues

In the remainder of this final chapter, I will discuss some other issues that are pertinent to the work presented in this book.

Pre-Session Form, Audio-Recording and Transcript

It is a feature of my[1] single-session work that I invite the person to prepare for the session in advance, and that I provide them with an audio recording and a transcript[2] of the session for later review. In the follow-up questionnaire, I asked volunteers for their views on these three features of my practice.

THE PRE-SESSION FORM

All volunteers who provided a response indicated that they found it helpful to complete a pre-session form. In

---

[1] While I recommend that therapists invite their clients to prepare for sessions, the use of audio-recordings and transcripts are a matter of personal preference.

[2] In my private SST work, I provide the audio recording free of charge, However, if someone wishes to receive the transcript, I kindly request that they cover the cost of transcription, which is carried out by a professional transcriber. In this book, both the audio recording and the transcript were provided free of charge.

response to the question, 'How helpful did you find the pre-session form if you were sent one? Please elaborate', volunteers said the following:

- 'Helpful in the sense I knew what example to bring to session. However, I typically allow for a natural in the moment process when thinking about emotionally charged experiences. Considering it was one session, it definitely prevented wasting time so we could dive straight in' (Sarah Louise, Chapter 2)

- 'I found this helpful as it gave me time to think in depth about my issue before the session. I also believe it gave Windy an insight into the problem so it was helpful to establish a sense of mutual understanding within the therapeutic relationship' (Ruth, Chapter 3)

- 'Very helpful for clarifying for myself exactly what I needed to work on in the session and enabling me to come well prepared. I think it saved wasting some of the actual session time and thus maximised its efficiency' (Cat, Chapter 4)

- 'It was helpful to know what to expect from the session' (Sylvia, Chapter 5)

- No response (Louise, Chapter 6)

- 'I found the form helpful. It was quite affronting (sic) to write down issues in this way and I did feel vulnerable sending it off – it felt like a real commitment to discuss the problem head-on, one which I felt ashamed about, so no turning back! But I liked that a lot as it felt it required courage and commitment from me' (Lily, Chapter 7)

- 'The pre-session was helpful as it encouraged me to reflect and get to the heart of the issue. This helped to fend off lots of other thoughts coming in which can create diversions/blockers.

  The form reminded me of my journalism training. When you have a news story to write, with lots of information, we were challenged to imagine that you have just met a friend who you need to convey the core of the story to in around 25 words. This would be your introduction from which the rest of the story would flow' (Lottie, Chapter 8).

- 'I found the pre-session form helpful to consolidate my thoughts before attending. Without it I could have spent the hour trying to create a context. It helped me be concise and prepared for attending' (Helen, Chapter 9)

AUDIO-RECORDING

Directly after the session, I sent volunteers a link for them to download an audio-recording of the session for their later review. Four of the volunteers found listening to the audio recording helpful, very helpful or extremely helpful, one found it unhelpful, and two hadn't listened to it. Of these two, one planned to do so if necessary, while the other did not want to listen to it. Finally, one volunteer mistakenly thought I had sent a link to the video, which they had no intention of watching. This is what volunteers had to say about the recording and their use of it in their follow-up questionnaire.

- 'I haven't listened to this yet as I have a clear enough memory of our session, and have retained the areas important for me to take forward. I think it is valuable to have considering it is one session, as I may look back over it and it would be especially helpful if I'd not had much therapy previously' (Sarah Louise, Chapter 2)

- 'I found the audio-recording extremely helpful, as I listened to the content of the session in the days following, and was able to process my feelings and take action'. (Ruth, Chapter 3)

- 'Very helpful because I found I could not remember much detail of the session until I listened back to it carefully. It was a useful means for reflection on the session' (Cat, Chapter 4)

- 'I do not personally find the audio helpful, I much prefer using a transcript, since it allows me to extrapolate and highlight quickly some poignant sentences or text that otherwise I might miss while listening. I personally feel like seeing things written down makes some concepts "sink in" more' (Sylvia, Chapter 5)

- 'I feel the recording was very helpful, as there were parts I had forgotten' (Louise, Chapter 6)

- 'I didn't listen to the audio recording, I would prefer not to!' (Lily, Chapter 7)

- 'The recording was helpful as it allowed me to reflect back on the issue. Sometimes, in the moment, it can be difficult to remember all exchanges in the therapy room. As this was single-session therapy, following up for clarification is not as easy as it would be with weekly sessions.' (Lottie, Chapter 8)

- I didn't re-watch the video, I find it hard to watch myself on video (Helen, Chapter 9)[3]

TRANSCRIPT

A week after the session, I sent all volunteers a written transcript of the session for their later review. Five people found reading the transcript helpful or very helpful, one person found it a little helpful, one person didn't find it helpful or unhelpful, and one person hadn't read it yet but may do so in future.

- 'I haven't read this yet as I have a clear enough memory of our session, and have retained the areas important for me to take forward. I think it is valuable to have considering it is one session, as I may look back over it and it would be especially helpful if I'd not had much therapy previously' (Sarah Louise, Chapter 2).

- 'I found it a little helpful, although it did not take into account the humour within the session' (Ruth, Chapter 3).

- 'Very helpful because I found I could not remember much detail of the session until I listened back to it carefully. It was a useful means for reflection on the session' (Cat, Chapter 4)

- 'The transcript was very helpful' (Sylvia, Chapter 5)

- 'Once again, helpful to see how session flowed' (Louise, Chapter 6)

---

[3] I sent all volunteers a download link for the audio recording of the session. Helen was mistaken on this point.

- 'I had a read of the transcript and didn't find it helpful or unhelpful' (Lily, Chapter 7)

- 'The transcript (was helpful). It also allowed me to go back on points even quicker than the audio-recording' (Lottie, Chapter 8)

- 'It was helpful to re-read over the dialogue' (Helen, Chapter 9)

My Appraisal of My Work in the Sessions

In all of the eight transcripts presented in this book, I have provided an ongoing commentary on what I was doing and the reasons for my interventions. I have not held back from being critical of my work. In this section, I will give an overview of my work across these eight sessions.

FOCUS

I believe a major strength of my single-session work, evident across all eight sessions, is that I can agree on a focus for the session with the person and help them maintain this focus. I think my work with Lottie (see Chapter 8) is a good example of this.

GOAL-DIRECTED

In single-session therapy, we typically do not work with a client so that their problem becomes a non-problem by the end of the session. Instead, we work to help them take away something that they can use later to aid problem resolution. In doing this, we encourage them to set session goals. I usually am good at helping clients to set session goals, but I failed to do so with sufficient clarity in my work with Lily (Chapter 7), Lottie (Chapter 8) and Helen (Chapter 9).

CLARITY

Normally, one of the features of my single-session work is that I am clear. Indeed, Sylvia (Chapter 5) noted that the clear and concise way I explained things was a particularly helpful factor for her. However, there were other times that I was not as clear as I could have been. This was due to me bringing together two or more concepts in my conversation with a person, which ended up confusing rather than clarifying matters. My work with Sarah Louise (Chapter 2) is a good example of my lack of clarity, which stems from trying to cover too much ground.

One of the ways I ensure clarity is by asking individuals to share their understanding of a concept I've introduced, taking care to indicate that I'm doing so to determine whether I've been clear rather than testing them. For example, with Sylvia, I distinguish between ego hurt and poor me hurt, but don't check with her whether this distinction is clear to her or whether it is helpful to her

LESS IS MORE

One of my personal vulnerabilities as a single-session therapist is that at times, I cover too much ground in a session, with the result that the person takes away less on specific issues than they would do if I adhered to the 'less is more' principle that is a feature of single-session work. My work with Sarah Louise (Chapter 2) is a good example of what not to do in a single session. on this point. Conversely, my sessions with Ruth (Chapter 3) and Cat

(Chapter 4) are good examples of me working with people when I didn't cover too much ground. Both sessions show that important themes can emerge from a focused conversation in a relaxed way when the therapist is not trying to do too much.

UNDERSTANDING THE CONTEXT

Some people believe that, as there is a lot to do in a single session, there is insufficient time to understand the context of an issue. I disagree with this, and my work with Sylvia (Chapter 5) demonstrates this. I spend the first half of the session getting a clear understanding of the problem-in-context and the second half looking for a way to help Sylvia to get unstuck. The understanding that I derived helped me to see that Sylvia had not fully addressed her feelings of hurt about being rejected by her two friends.

CLIENT-LED

A significant feature of single-session work is that it should be client-led rather than therapist-led. Helping sessions to be client-led involves the therapist in asking the client to take the lead on important decisions rather than making these decisions for the client, A good example where I needed to be client-led in my thinking occurred in my session with Louise (see Chapter 6). Louise had sought help for her feelings of self-doubt and fear of failure, which showed up in two areas of her life: procrastinating on her studies and not committing to her relationship. In the session, we dealt with both. However, I made the judgement to switch from the first issue to the second. It would have been better if I had asked Louise if there was more we could have done on the first issue before unilaterally deciding to move onto the second. This would have been more client-led.

Another area where the issue of the therapist leading the session becomes significant in SST concerns the introduction of concepts derived from their own therapeutic allegiances and how this should be managed, if at all. My approach to this subject is that my primary goal is to help the client address their issue by utilising factors that are already within their repertoire but perhaps hidden from view. This occurred particularly in my work with Ruth (Chapter 3) and Cat (Chapter 4). Then, if I need to introduce other therapeutic concepts, I will do so, but only after asking the person if they are interested in my 'take', as I did in my work with Sylvia (Chapter 5). I am pleased with how I did this, as evidenced in the following exchange:

Windy: And hurt and sadness are about somewhat different things. There are two types of hurt. Would you mind if I gave you my 'take' on hurt?

Sylvia: Please, absolutely. That's why I'm here.

Elsewhere in the session, I was less inviting in introducing concepts informed by REBT theory (e.g., my work with Helen in Chapter 9)

GETTING TO THE HEART OF THE MATTER

I think that the power of single-session therapy resides in the therapist and client getting to the heart of the matter and working to introduce some meaningful novelty at that level. I think that I did this in my work with Sylvia (Chapter 5). In other sessions, there may have been themes that were important to work with. For example, Ruth (Chapter 3) mentioned a fear of conflict, but the fact that we did not address it did not seem to be a concern for her. Similarly, I did not adequately deal with Cat's sense of self-protection (Chapter 4), but, I think we covered this in a more general way when we spoke about dealing with obstacles.

Perhaps the clearest example of my failure to get to the heart of the matter was with Helen (Chapter 9). This would have involved addressing that part of Helen that still longed to have her emotional needs met by her mother, even though from a realistic perspective this was unlikely to happen. While I recognised and worked with Helen's sadness and grief, I did not identify and work with her feelings of hurt, which, as I see it now, lay beneath her anger towards her mother. Now, I may be in error about this, but I wish I had created the opportunity to discuss it with Helen. As I explained in Chapter 9, I wrote to Helen about this ang published her reply. I reproduce the relevant part of it here.

I think you're right that there's hurt underneath. It's been pushed down for so long as a form of self-protection that it can feel almost out of reach. Maybe that part of me would have benefited from being seen more clearly in the room, although reading back over the transcript and your reflections did bring a tear to my eye. Your noticing of that hurt part now helps it feel a little more seen and validated. So – thank you!'

CREATIVITY AND HUMOUR

I like bringing humour and creativity to my work as a single-session therapist, and there are instances when I did this in the sessions presented in this book. Ruth (Chapter 3) mentioned my humour as a therapeutic factor and the fact that she and her friends all carry red flags to indicate when she is getting back into her unhealthy relationship pattern. I have three favourite props that I use in single-session work – a red flag to indicate that something isn't healthy for the person, a magic wand to bring about change that is not within the person's control, but which can be achieved without effort and a crystal ball to tell the future. I used the red flag in my work with Ruth (Chapter 3) and Lily (Chapter 7) and the magic wand with Louise (Chapter 6) and Helen (Chapter 9). All four people referenced its use positively in their feedback questionnaire.

A Final Caveat

I view single-session therapy as a mode of therapy delivery where the therapist and client agree to meet for a session, collaborating to help the client achieve what they hope to accomplish during the session. After a period of reflecting on what they have learned from the session, digesting this learning, and implementing it, the client decides whether or not they need further help, which is available should they choose to access it.

The work described and discussed in this book differs from the above in one crucial respect. The volunteer and I agreed to have only one session, a restriction they were aware of before signing up for the session. If further assistance were made available to the volunteers, it would be interesting to speculate on how many of them would have accessed it and what the impact of such help would have been on their progress ratings.

Conclusion

I have been quite critical of some of my therapeutic work presented in this book. In some ways, my work fell short of the standard to which I aspire. However, I am not ashamed of revealing my work to you. Indeed, I am happy to show my work warts and all. Hopefully, this will demonstrate that so-called 'experts' are not infallible and can make fundamental errors. However, despite my errors, all volunteers made some progress in freeing themselves from the issue with which they were stuck, and this freeing process was not dependent on the absence of these errors. It is worthwhile remembering that what the person takes away from the single session is mediated by their strengths and prior ways of helping themself as much or even more than it is mediated by my skill. This does not mean that therapist skills do not matter. They do. It means that people will benefit from your work if your work is 'good enough'. At the end of the day, while far from perfect, the work I did with the volunteers was good enough to allow them to take away what most of them had come for.

References

Bordin, E.S. (1979). The generalizability of the psychoanalytic concept of the working alliance. *Psychotherapy: Theory, Research and Practice, 16*(3): 252–260.

Brown, G.S., & Jones, E.R. (2005). Implementation of a feedback system in a managed care environment: What are patients teaching us. *Journal of Clinical Psychology/In Session, 61.* 187–198.

Cooper, S.J. (2024). *Brief Narrative Practice in Single-Session Therapy.* Routledge.

Dryden, W. (2011). *Counselling in a Nutshell. 2nd Edition.* Sage.

Dryden, W. (2022). *Single-Session Therapy: Responses to Frequently Asked Questions.* Routledge.

Dryden, W. (2025a). Bringing a single-session mindset to counselling in an online health service in the UK. In F. Cannistrà, & M.F. Hoyt (eds), *Single Session Therapies: Why and How One-At-A-Time Mindsets Are Effective* (pp. 124–136). Routledge.

Dryden, W. (2025b). *A Critical Examination of Irvin D. Yalom's Single-Session Consultations: It Is the Relationship that Heals.* Routledge.

Frank, J.D. (1961). *Persuasion and Healing: A Comparative Study of Psychotherapy.* The Johns Hopkins Press.

Hoyt, M.F., Young, J., & Rycroft, P. (eds) (2021). *Single Session Thinking and Practice in Global, Cultural, and Familial Contexts: Expanding Applications.* Routledge.

Pugh, M. (2024). Single-session chairwork: Overview and case illustration of brief dialogical psychotherapy. *British Journal of Guidance and Counselling, 52*(4), 777–795.

Simon, G. E., Imel, Z. E., Ludman, E.J. & Steinfeld, B.J. (2012). Is dropout after a first psychotherapy visit always a bad outcome? *Psychiatric Services, 63*(7), 705–707.

Yalom, I.D., & Yalom, B. (2024). *Hour of the Heart: Connecting in the Here and Now.* Piatkus.

Young, J. (2018). SST: The misunderstood gift that keeps on giving. In M.F. Hoyt, M. Bobele, A. Slive, J. Young & M. Talmon (eds), *Single-Session Therapy by Walk-In or Appointment: Administrative, Clinical, and Supervisory Aspects of One-at-a-Time Services* (pp. 40–58). Routledge.

Index

Index

www.ingramcontent.com/pod-product-compliance
Lightning Source LLC
Chambersburg PA
CBHW071220290326
41931CB00037B/1504